A Memory of Trains

A Memory of Trains

The Boll Weevil and Others

Text and photographs by **Louis D. Rubin, Jr.**

UNIVERSITY OF SOUTH CAROLINA PRESS

Published in Columbia, South Carolina, by the
University of South Carolina Press

Manufactured in the United States of America

04   03   02   01   00   5   4   3   2   1

Library of Congress Cataloging-in-Publication Data

Rubin, Louis Decimus, 1923–
    A memory of trains : the Boll Weevil and others / text
and photographs by Louis D. Rubin, Jr.
      p. cm.
    Includes bibliographical references.
    ISBN 1-57003-382-X (cloth : alk. paper)
    1. Railroads—United States—Pictorial works.   I. Title.
TF23.R83   2000
385'.0975—dc21   00-009043

Frontispiece: The Chesapeake and Ohio Sportsman, with a
4–8–4 Greenbrier locomotive at the head, at Waynesboro,
Virginia, December 1947

for John F. Harrington
in sixty years of friendship

Contents

Illustrations

Prefatory Note

From 1946 through the mid-1950s it was my habit to spend a good deal of my leisure time watching and riding aboard railroad trains. Before then, as a child and youth, I had always liked trains, and I have never afterward lost interest in them. But during those years, when I was in my twenties and early thirties, I traveled considerable distances to see them, photographed them, and wrote newspaper and magazine articles about them.

Recently I happened upon a number of those photographs. Most, though not all, are of steam locomotives, and it occurred to me that, while by no means unique, they comprise something of a visual record of an important era in American railroad history: the end of the age of steam and its supersession by diesel power, and the swift decline of intercity passenger travel by rail after World War II as long-distance automobile and airline travel took over. So I determined to publish some of them as a book, with an accompanying text.

All the photographs but one are my own. The cameras used were mainly an ancient Argus with a defective lens; a Korelle; a Kodak Retina, all of these 35mm; and occasionally a couple of better, borrowed cameras. At no time did I ever have access to darkroom equipment; all were developed and printed commercially. Most of the negatives have been lost, while the prints, being approximately a half century or more old, have turned sallow and faded with age, so that it was necessary for the majority of them to be copied, sometimes enlarged, and frequently restored digitally.

This is mainly a Southeastern and Middle Atlantic states book. That was where I was living and working when I was taking railroad photographs. There are some Midwestern and Western trains, but not many, for the simple reason that when I visited those parts of the country I did so mainly aboard trains, and as all railfans know, that was not the way to get good train pictures. You needed to station yourself at a strategic junction point somewhere along the main line and wait for the trains to come by, not be riding aboard the train.

The sole photograph of a train not taken by me appears here because of all the trains remembered and written about, this one was of greatest importance for me. That I was *not* able to photograph it for myself is central to the experience here recorded.

In the accompanying text I have tried to tell about the trains I once knew, and, here and there in the narrative, to suggest what they meant for me at the time. For in retrospect it seems clear that along with the inherent interest of trains and railroading that was always present for me and indeed still is, during the years that I write of they possessed an imaginative and symbolic importance having to do with various matters, including the search for what turned out to be a vocation. It was a complex business, and I am far from insisting that what was true for me applies to all or even most train buffs. But in my instance there were connections, some of which I have sought to suggest, and some of which can just go without saying.

I am all too aware that I have produced a document offering less about the specifics of trains and railroading than dedicated railfans might prefer, while for general readers it includes what will doubtless seem far too much material about certain devices of transportation equipment that ceased to function some decades ago, and in memory are important only to myself. If the text that follows does not find favor, I can only hope that the photographs themselves will take up some of the slack.

Louis D. Rubin, Jr.
Chapel Hill, North Carolina
June 10, 1999

Acknowledgments

To George Kennedy, of Fort Collins, Colorado, emeritus professor of classics at the University of North Carolina at Chapel Hill and a lifetime train buff and railroad historian, I am indebted for a critical reading of this manuscript that saved me from what would have been numerous embarrassing errors of memory and interpretation.

For the picture of the Boll Weevil, the one essential photograph in this book and the only one in it not taken by myself, I thank a lifelong friend, William D. Chamberlain, and his son, David Chamberlain, both of Charleston, South Carolina.

The Center for Teaching and Learning and the Map Collection of the Wilson Library of the University of North Carolina at Chapel Hill generously joined forces to provide the several maps contained in this book.

Anne Winslow utilized the resources of digital computer technology to restore or enhance the visibility of the foxed and fading images of photographs taken a half-century earlier.

For information about various of the locomotives herein depicted I am grateful to H. Warren Middleton, N&W Historical Society, Forest, Va.; Lee Gordon, Louisville and Nashville Historical Society; Jim Q. Kubajak, Illinois Central Historical Society; Capt. John Le Cato, Charleston, S.C.; Larry Goolsby, Atlantic Coast Line and Seaboard Air Line Railroads Historical Society; J. P. Terp, Sr., Philipsburg Railroad Historians, Philipsburg, N.J.; and Robert A. Creamer, Tuckahoe, N.Y.

Throughout the writing and preparation of this book Robert Alden Rubin has kept his elderly father on track editorially, and rescued him and his manuscript from numerous near-fatal computer crashes.

A Memory of Trains

One Prologue
A Smudge of Smoke

(All the coaches shall be scrap and rust and all the men and
women laughing in the diners and sleepers shall pass to ashes.)
—Carl Sandburg, "Limited"

There is a place on U. S. Highway One, about ten miles north of Rockingham, North Carolina, where the road runs parallel to the main-line railroad tracks. Whenever I drive along it a smudge of gray smoke is in sight above a stand of trees to the north.

My response is instant and reflexive: *A train is coming!*

It takes me only a moment to realize that no railroad train is in fact coming down the tracks—and that even if it were, the dark smoke I see could have nothing to do with it. Any train now operating there, en route to or from the CSX yards at Hamlet twelve miles down the line, would be powered by a diesel locomotive, and whatever thin trace of smoke emanating from it would certainly not be rising above the grove of trees and spreading over the nearby sky in the way that coal smoke from a steam locomotive would do.

I have only to drive on for another mile or so, and the source of the smoke will become evident: a mill. Still, until I actually see where the smoke is coming from, there is always the hope that a train will appear.

———

The steam locomotives are long since gone from the railroads. The few that have survived do so as exhibits in parks and museums, on occasion hauling railfan excursions, or else as tourist attractions in the mountains. Diesel locomotives have otherwise totally replaced them on American railroads, and indeed just about all over the world. What has been lost with their passing? Other than as pure nostalgia, the sentimental regret for days gone by, why should anyone care? Why do my senses quicken and my attention still turn instantly alert because of the accidental congruence of steel rails along a highway and smoke up ahead?

It is because steam trains were *beautiful.* Not that there was anything tranquil and serene about the beauty. Their attractiveness had to do with power and energy. All the machinery was on the outside, and when they came pounding along the rails, drive wheels turning, drive rods stroking, pistons exploding with sound and fury and sending a swirling cloud of bituminous coal smoke overhead, the ground shook. There was the sense of tremendous force harnessed for a utilitarian purpose, that somehow did not contain the sum total of their imaginative presence. There was excess—which translated into an emotional and aesthetic experience. One saw the train, one heard it and smelled it, and one felt it—not only in the sense of the earth trembling and the wind rushing by as it passed, but as an experience involving the assertion of singularity, the display of strength and a capacity for distances: the achievement of spectacle.

Their hold upon the imagination was evocative and allusive. Good poems were written about seeing them in motion. Ballads were sung about them. Their imagery pervaded our speech: *express-train speed, asleep at the switch, milk run, whistle-stop, jerkwater town, main line, trunk line, railroaded, derail, mile-a-minute, hot box, caught on the tracks, from across the tracks, the wrong side of the tracks, sidetracked, untracked, full throttle, getting up steam, a head of steam, blowing off steam, wrecking crew, deadhead, sideswipe, flag down, the long haul, hauling the mail, a slow drag, highballing it, a roundhouse punch, making smoke, pouring on the coal, clickety-clack, nonstop, doubleheader.*

The sounds of their coming and going were unmistakable and unforgettable. The chuff-chuff-chuff of a mountain locomotive laboring its way up a steep grade conferred order and emphasis upon the darkness.

The wail of a steam locomotive whistle, heard at night through an open window, was like no other. A working locomotive blowing for grade crossings, with the low rumble of flanged wheels on steel rails, spoke to the loneliness of the young. It made them want to go along wherever the train might be bound.

To someone growing up in a big city this may not have been true, or if so perhaps only very late at night when the urban clamor subsided and faint train whistles might be heard on the far outskirts. But to persons raised out in the provinces, in small cities and towns or in the countryside anywhere within miles of a railroad, trains were everywhere to be heard, going places.

It is of that time that I shall be telling.

Two The Seaboard Yards

Toad sat straight down in the middle of the dusty road, his legs stretched out before him, and stared fixedly in the direction of the disappearing motorcar. He breathed short, his face wore a placid, satisfied expression, and at intervals he faintly murmured, "Pooppoop!"

—Kenneth Grahame, *The Wind in the Willows*

Then felt I like some watcher of the skies
When a new planet swims into his ken.

—John Keats, "On First Looking
into Chapman's Homer"

I do not have a photograph of the train I rode when I got out of the Army at the end of January 1946. I had been stationed at Fort Benning, near Columbus, Georgia. The Separation Center was at Camp Gordon, near Augusta. With my severance pay and a gold "ruptured duck" emblem sewn upon my uniform shirt and blouse to denote my ex-GI status, I caught a Delta airliner over to Columbia, South Carolina, to spend the night with my aunt and uncle. The next day I bought a tweed jacket and a necktie with a pattern on it, and ordered a suit of civilian clothes from my uncle, who was a tailor. That evening I boarded the train, bound for my parents' home in Richmond, Virginia.

It had been my intention, once out of the Army, to return to Charleston, South Carolina, where I had grown up, and take my senior year at the College of Charleston. But my discharge had come abruptly, the second school term would be underway within a couple of days, and there was no time to arrange it. So I would go back and finish up at the University of Richmond.

The train was the Seaboard Air Line's Silver Meteor. It pulled into the station in Columbia behind a three-unit diesel-electric locomotive, a long train of mostly streamlined stainless steel coaches but with several older cars in its consist as well, for like all rail-

road trains it was well patronized. The war had been over for five months, but seating space on trains remained in heavy demand. I was fortunate to have been able to get a reservation on such short notice.

After I found my seat in the darkened coach and settled back in the reclining chair, I halfway hoped that a couple of MPs would come along, espy the green sports coat and necktie that I had bought in Columbia and was wearing with my uniform blouse, and demand to know what I was doing out of uniform. I would throw open my coat, show them my gold ruptured duck, and bid them be on their way.

———

When I think back on wartime railroading, an image comes to mind. It is late at night, and I am aboard a coach on another train, somewhere between Richmond and Atlanta, returning to Fort Benning after a furlough. Every seat on the coach is taken, and there is luggage stacked along the corridors. Sometime in the night I get up to go to the men's room. In the dim light I pass a soldier, a man in his thirties, obviously well liquored. He is standing in the corridor, staggering to keep his feet as the car lurches, and, oblivious to his surroundings, he is pissing on the suitcases.

It was not usually as unpleasant as that. But during the war the railroads were taxed to their utmost capacity. The lean years of the Depression were over. There was a tremendous increase both in freight and passenger traffic. Something like a million men a month were transported in troop trains alone. Passenger travel, which had been falling off steadily during the 1920s and 1930s because of competition from automobiles and buses, now underwent a considerable expansion. For the first time in decades, railroads began turning a profit on passenger service.

As might be expected, there was a severe shortage of operating equipment, and the enormous industrial requirements of global war meant that there were restrictions upon the manufacture of new locomotives and rolling stock. Equipment that would otherwise have been scrapped stayed in use. Steam locomotives that had been relegated to branch line and switching duties were seen hauling main-line freight trains once again. Day coaches were crowded, with passengers often forced to stand in the aisles. Reservations in the Pullman sleeper cars were not always available. Throngs of outbound travelers crowded about the train gates at all the major stations, waiting for the announcements that would allow them to hurry to the train platforms and aboard the coaches in search of seats. The odds were always that trains would be late arriving and departing. To alleviate the shortage of Pullman cars, some freight cars were even remodeled and berths installed in them for use on troop trains. I once traveled from Grand Central Terminal in New York City to Pine Camp (now Fort Drum), in Watertown, New York, aboard such a car; it was a rough, windowless nighttime ride.

More often on overnight runs, enlisted personnel simply endured hard, upright seats. After basic infantry training in Alabama in the summer of 1943 I was part of a group of several dozen men sent to New Haven, Connecticut, for Italian language training at Yale University. We were loaded into an old day coach one morning and off we went. The air-conditioning worked only very imperfectly. When nighttime arrived, we discovered that it was possible to lift the seat backs out of their sockets and wedge them between the seats, thus providing a flat surface that, whatever its rigidity, was no more uncomfortable than sleeping on the ground under shelter tents, which we had been doing for the two weeks previous to our entraining. (Upon arriving in New Haven the next afternoon we were marched over to the Yale campus and assigned to dormitory rooms, which as far as most of us were concerned was the equivalent of checking into the Waldorf-Astoria.)

That was in 1943. In January of 1946, the crunch was only just beginning to ease. Several million armed forces personnel had been discharged by then, but there were millions more to go, and a vast amount of traveling around still remained to be done, principally by rail, before the country could settle down to peacetime existence again.

———

Two hours after leaving Columbia the Silver Meteor arrived in Hamlet, just across the state line, where the trains changed crews. It was in Hamlet that the Seaboard's two main lines were united, one from Atlanta and Birmingham, the other from Florida, for the run to Richmond and Washington. I stepped out onto the station platform. I was looking for a certain little train I remembered from when I was a boy, hoping to catch a glimpse of it somewhere around. I knew that it operated between Hamlet and Savannah on a branch line of the Seaboard running through Charleston. It was a gas-electric combine called the Boll Weevil, and all during my years in Charleston I had seen it coming and going, or else waiting, seemingly forever, at the Seaboard station near Hampton Park.

On furloughs home to Richmond from Fort Benning I had come through Hamlet several times and had looked for it, but without success. This time, however, I thought that I did see it, across from the station, a silhouette in the darkness standing on a sidetrack next to a warehouse, waiting for morning and the run down to Charleston, 160 miles away. If so, I did not have the chance to get a closer look at it, for another Seaboard passenger train came rolling into the station and screened off my view.

It was ironic that it was the gas-electric doodlebug, and not the streamlined main-line train, that I now wanted to see, because when I was a youth growing up in Charleston the little train had seemed to me the very epitome of small-time, humdrum mediocrity. The train that had interested me then, and stirred my imagination with thoughts of escape to the North, was the Havana Special, which stopped at the North Charleston station of the Atlantic Coast Line before continuing on Richmond, Washington, and the Northeast—and, a little later, the two streamliners, the East and West Coast Champions. In the late 1930s various railroads had turned to diesel-electric locomotives and stainless-steel coaches for their showcase passenger trains. The Atlantic Coast Line introduced the reserved-seat Champions, and the Seaboard the Silver Meteor and Silver Star, which did not come through Charleston but crossed South Carolina further upcountry, via Columbia. With their long strings of silver coaches and their powerful new diesel locomotives, those were the glamour trains. Yet there I was, straining to catch sight of the Boll Weevil, and feeling a pang of disappointment when the streamliner came along to block it from sight.

———

I graduated from the University of Richmond the following August. I had gotten myself engaged to be married to a girl from Teaneck, New Jersey, and found a job as a reporter on the *Bergen Evening Record*, a newspaper in Hackensack, across the river from Teaneck. Since childhood there had never been any question in my mind about what I wanted to do once I finished college. I would be a newspaperman. I might also do other kinds of writing—novels, plays—but it was journalism that I was set upon, and a position on the staff of a daily newspaper. My experience in the Army,

where toward the end of my time at Fort Benning I had worked for the camp newspaper, had only whetted my appetite. Now the long wait would be over, and I would begin my career.

A couple of weeks before graduation I noticed a magazine on display at a newsstand, and I bought a copy. It was published in Milwaukee, Wisconsin, and bore the title of *Trains*. My interest in the subject was of long standing. As a child in Charleston I used to pick up timetables at the train station, bring them home, and read them over and over. I knew the route and the destination of every passenger train that came through the city. When my family moved to Richmond, the year before I was inducted into the Army, I sometimes went down to the Broad Street Station on Sunday afternoons to watch the trains arriving and departing. While stationed at Fort Benning, on the occasions when I got furloughs or three-day passes I liked to arrive at the station in Columbus well before train time so that I could sit outside and watch the locomotives come and go.

Yet for all my considerable interest in railroads, until I purchased and began reading that magazine I had not realized that there were specific types of steam locomotives, and that it was possible to identify and to distinguish between them by the number and variety of the drive- and truck-wheels that were visible on either side. A "Mikado" locomotive, for example, was classified as a 2–8–2 because it had two pilot truck wheels, eight drive wheels, and two trailing truck wheels: <o OOOO o. A 4–6–2 "Pacific" had four pilot truck wheels, six drive wheels, and two trailing truck wheels: <oo OOO o. A 2–8–0 "Consolidation" had two pilot truck wheels, eight drive wheels, and no trailing truck wheels: <o OOOO. There were locomotives called Mallets, used for pulling trains on steep grades, which had double sets of drive wheels. And so on. (There was no particular logic to the naming. A 2–8–2 was called a Mikado because the first one was built for use in Japan. The first 4–6–2 Pacific was originally designed for a railroad in New Zealand. A 2–8–0 was

called a Consolidation because the first such was built by the Lehigh Valley Railroad immediately after a merger with a number of feeder lines. Mallets were named for their French inventor, Anatole Mallet.)

More than that, I saw that there must be many thousands of other people who had an interest similar to my own, enough of them to make up the circulation of a national magazine devoted entirely to railroading and written from the standpoint not of a trade journal for trainmen but of persons who merely enjoyed watching trains and locomotives in action.

Before I read that copy of *Trains Magazine* my interest in railroads and railroading had been more or less random and, in more than one sense, unfocused. Much though I enjoyed riding on trains, it had not occurred to me that taking photographs of them could be a specific kind of avocation, an activity to be engaged in deliberately and consciously, in the same way that one might build model airplanes, play golf, watch baseball, or collect stamps.

The next afternoon I borrowed my father's camera, rode the Westhampton street car down to within walking distance of Richmond's Hermitage Yards, and found my way to a point on the bridge over the tracks. I watched as locomotives and trains came along, freight and passenger both, to and from the Broad Street and Main Street stations, outbound and inbound along the main lines to the North and the South. The Seaboard yards were located just below where I was standing, and there was a 2–8–2 locomotive across the way, its smoke box elaborately gusseted up with tanks and valves. Beyond it was a Seaboard road diesel. I made my way down an embankment and across the tracks, and began taking photographs. Thereafter, and for at least the next ten years of my life, I was firmly hooked.

Three Foray and Return

"Do you know why you are going, or are you just taking a ride on the train?"—Thomas Wolfe, *Look Homeward, Angel*

From the standpoint of being able to see and photograph numbers and varieties of railroad locomotives, living and working in northern New Jersey across from New York City, as I did when I moved there in September of 1946, was made to order. The New York Central's West Shore Division tracks lay immediately behind my girlfriend's home. It operated along the Hudson River from Weehawken to Albany, with numerous freight trains, a few through passenger trains, and a host of commutation trains, all steam-powered. The Erie, the Delaware, Lackawanna and Western, the Central Railway of New Jersey, the Lehigh Valley, the Baltimore and Ohio, and the Reading likewise had passenger trains terminating at the ferry terminals along the river. The Pennsylvania's electrified main line from Washington ran from Newark across the Jersey Meadows to the tunnel under the Hudson, with its clockers—New York City to Philadelphia, every hour on the hour, both ways—and other trains in constant processional.

The area was honeycombed with commuter runs, including two that served Hackensack, where I lived. The New York, Susquehanna and Western operated little cars, similar in size to the Boll Weevil back in Charleston but far more modern and streamlined, which terminated at Susquehanna Transfer, behind Union City close to the Pennsylvania tunnel entrance. There passengers boarded buses that took them through the Lincoln Tunnel into Manhattan. The New Jersey and New York and the Northern Railroad of New Jersey, subsidiaries of the Erie, operated commuter trains pulled by antique "ten-wheelers"

(4–6–0) and "Atlantics" (4–4–2) with very high drive wheels, which delivered their commuter passengers to the ferryboats at the Erie Terminal in Jersey City.

The 4–6–2 "Pacific" commuter locomotives on the Central's West Shore Division were almost as old, dating back to World War I days. Weekday mornings and late afternoons they came along the multi-track line in rapid procession. My girlfriend's home was located about midway between the Teaneck and West Englewood stations, which were little more than a mile apart. From the tracks behind her house I could make out the trains as they left one station and when they arrived at the other. With an old 35mm Argus camera that I bought for ten dollars, I sometimes took up station between the double sets of tracks, photographing trains as they came by. There was ample room there and I was in no danger, but my presence clearly annoyed some of the train crews, for once as a locomotive neared someone held a water hose out of the cab, and before I knew what was happening I was nicely wetted down.

I soon grew so accustomed to the old commuter locomotives passing by that I ceased to photograph them. What I always hoped to see was one of the occasional through trains, which ran all the way to Albany and were pulled by the Central's newer and considerably more powerful 4–6–4 "Hudsons," or freight trains with 4–8–2 "Mohawk" (on other railroads called a "Mountain") locomotives at the head. The Mohawks had smoke deflectors alongside the sides of the smoke box, in the style of European locomotives.

One afternoon I happened to be watching when an unusual spectacle turned up. A 4–8–2 locomotive came along with a string of gleaming new 2–8–4 steam locomotives in tow. They had shields that angled over the sides of the head end, and other features that were unlike those on any locomotives I had ever seen. I learned later that they had been manufactured by the American Locomotive Company in Schenectady and were destined for shipment to the French National Railways, to replace locomotives destroyed during the Allied invasion of Europe two years before.

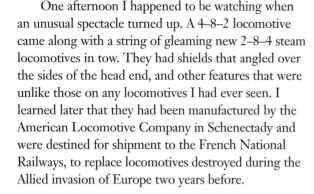

———

Except for my winter in the Army this was my first foray into the North, and my Charleston accent was a source of much merriment in the newsroom. My interest in trains also amused some of the reporters and desk men on the newspaper, but the associate editor liked trains, and when I showed him some of the photographs I was taking, several times he loaned me his Voigtlander Bessa, a far better and more reliable camera than my old Argus, to take on my expeditions.

After a month of working in the newsroom I was assigned to cover the town of Teaneck, a "bedroom community" of 30,000, so called because the majority of its wage-earners commuted to New York City. Each morning I stopped in at the various municipal offices at the town hall and examined the police blotter. Then, unless there was a civic club luncheon to cover, there was usually little to do until the evenings, when the municipal court, the school board, and the town council sessions were held.

This left most of my afternoons free. I went into Manhattan one afternoon, took the ferry over to the Jersey Central terminal at Jersey City, walked out along the tracks to where the numerous tracks converged, and began photographing commuter trains as they emerged from the station. Most of them were pulled by little 4–6–0 "camelback" steam locomotives, with the operating cab located well up along the locomotive and the engineer's and fireman's stations separated by the

barrel of the boiler. The Lehigh Valley's commuter trains, one of them powered by a gas-electric combine like the Boll Weevils on the Seaboard back home and with elaborate zebra striping on the front, used adjacent trackage.

As the five o'clock going-home exodus began the trains came sailing by fast and furiously. Not all were commuter runs; a few were full-fledged intercity trains powered by 4–6–2 road locomotives. I snapped one picture after another, with the cathedral-like dome of the Jersey Central station and its steeple-style cupola for backdrop.

One Saturday morning I rode the little Susquehanna coach from Hackensack to the transfer near the entrance to the Pennsylvania Railway tunnel. Instead of boarding the bus to Manhattan I walked over to the Pennsylvania right-of-way, climbed up onto the embankment, and set out southward in the direction of Newark. I walked for a mile or so, photographing passing Pennsylvania GG-1 electric locomotives and multiple-unit commuter trains as I went, until I came to the Erie freight yards near Secaucus. There I climbed down to the Erie tracks and photographed several trains, including a 2–8–2 Mikado setting out westward with a long freight train. I walked westward to a commuter station, waited until an Erie gas-electric commuter coach came along, and rode several miles to Rutherford. I photographed more trains, then caught a bus back to Hackensack. On another occasion I took a Lackawanna train to the ferry terminal in Hoboken and photographed trains there from the head of the tracks.

It occurred to me that since daily trips to New York City and back occupied so important a place in the Bergen County scheme of things, I would develop a feature story about the New York Central's future plans for the West Shore Division's commuting service. As part of it, I arranged to get into a locomotive cab at the Teaneck station and go with it to Weehawken, where I would interview the division superintendent.

The inside of the old 4–6–2 locomotive cab was cramped. I sat next to the fireman on a raised seat, with the engineer on the right-hand side of the cab. It was a rough, swaying ride. From time to time the fireman scooped up shovelfuls of coal from the tender and in a single motion stepped on a pedal to open the doors of the firebox and flung the coal into the brightly burning interior. The division superintendent of motive power accompanied me and explained the working of the locomotive. Looking up the tracks I watched the guardrails swinging down and the automobiles pulling to a stop as we rolled through grade crossings.

At one point we passed a gray-painted road diesel-electric locomotive, northbound, ahead of a string of freight cars. "That's the O and W milk train," the superintendent told me. Each morning a railroad called the New York, Ontario and Western operated a train from the interior of New York State into Weehawken along the New York Central trackage, hauling milk. At Weehawken it dropped off its refrigerated boxcars, collected a string of empties, and headed back northward. It was the first diesel engine I had seen on the West Shore Division, or for that matter anywhere in the New York–New Jersey area.

Our train stopped at North Bergen, then went rumbling into a tunnel through the Palisades. It was dark, hot, and smoky in the open cab. A long several minutes went by before we emerged at the Central yards along the Hudson River. At an office in the wooden station building I interviewed the West Shore Division superintendent, then photographed some locomotives in the yards.

The trouble with my idea for the story was that although the superintendent uttered some generalities about possible future developments, the New York Central really had no plans or hopes for its West Shore Division commuter service other than to continue operating it as required by the Interstate Commerce Commission, using the same old locomotives and beat-up coaches.

———

What happened soon thereafter was that my girlfriend changed her mind, and I found myself with a returned engagement ring and a job I did not enjoy, in a place where, now that there was no specific reason to hold me there, I did not want to live. I missed the South. I decided to get out job inquiries to some of the South Carolina newspapers and to go back to Richmond. My foray northward having thus ended ingloriously, a few days later I was waiting at Penn Station in Manhattan for the next train to Washington.

The trip back South turned out to be a fitting denouement. At Washington I took a train on the Richmond, Fredericksburg and Potomac. It was February 1947, and that evening there were no throngs of outbound travelers waiting at the train gates. I was in the last day coach, at the end of the train, an old car with upright green-plush seats, similar to the car we had ridden overnight from Fort McClellan, Alabama, to New Haven during the war. Unlike the wartime trains, however, it was almost empty of passengers.

A half hour after the train left Fredericksburg it began to slacken speed, then slowed to a crawl. For the next fifteen minutes or so it alternated between creeping along slowly and halting, until at length it stopped moving altogether. I asked a trainman what was causing the delay. There was a wreck on the line up ahead, he said. No word had been received on how long it might take to clear the tracks.

After a while I walked back onto the open vestibule at the rear of the coach. The conductor and a brakeman were standing alongside the coach. It was a bitterly cold night, and their breath fogged as they talked. Further back along the tracks behind us a precautionary red warning flare was burning in the darkness.

I returned to my seat and resumed reading the book I had brought with me. The long delay continued. I tried to keep my mind on my book, but I kept thinking about what had happened, and the contrast between my high hopes of six months earlier and my present situation. I felt that a total defeat had been inflicted upon me. By then it was now close to eleven, and we were still far from Richmond and with no sign of the journey recommencing. The coach was getting uncomfortably warm. I went out onto the vestibule again. The conductor and brakeman were standing alongside. I stepped down the iron stairway and out onto the ground. Down the track, in place of the red warning flare, the headlamp of a stalled locomotive now shone. Behind it, further back, was the glow of another headlamp, and well back in the darkness, yet another. Up ahead, beyond the silhouette of the locomotive of our train, illuminated by its headlamp, were the rear vestibule lanterns of another passenger train.

What had happened, the brakeman said, was that a Chesapeake and Ohio freight train had jumped the tracks at the C&O crossing at Doswell, blocking the RF&P main line. In addition to the southbound trains waiting for the tracks to be cleared, of which ours was one of five, at least four northbound trains were idled on the far side of the crossing. The current estimate was that it would probably be at least another hour before the wrecking train now at work on the scene would be able to clear one of the tracks at the crossing, so that north-south traffic could resume.

It was after midnight when the whistle of a locomotive sounded, off in the darkness ahead. A few minutes later the tracks along the east side of our train were illuminated by a headlamp, and a northbound passenger train moved past. There was a lurch, and then at last I was headed south again.

Four Origins of an Obsession

Down at the station
Early in the morning . . .
　　—Children's song

The *News and Courier* in Charleston was contemplating adding a reporter. Charleston was where I had grown up. More than anyplace else, it was where I wanted to live.

I rode down on the Atlantic Coast Line's Havana Special. The train drew its name from the days when Henry M. Flagler had built Florida East Coast trackage all the way out to Key West, from where ferries could take passengers across the Gulf Stream to Cuba. The hurricane of 1935 destroyed much of the causeway along the Keys and the train thereafter went no further south than Miami, but the name remained unchanged. For as long as I could remember it had been arriving at North Charleston from Richmond and the North in the middle of the afternoon.

The northbound Special stopped by earlier in the day from Florida. As a child, when I imagined myself going up to New York City, where I had never been, it was always aboard the Havana Special. Even after the Coast Line introduced its East Coast and West Coast Champions, with streamlined coaches and diesel-electric locomotives, in the late 1930s, when I thought of traveling northward and careerward it was as a passenger on the Havana Special.

At Rocky Mount, North Carolina, the train changed crews, and I walked up the tracks and photographed the pair of purple-and-silver diesel-electric locomotives at its head. From having traveled to and from Charleston and Richmond, I knew the stops along the route very well. The closer we got to

Charleston the more there was to recognize and remember.

———

In my childhood there were three railroads in Charleston, each different from the others. They constituted a hierarchy, with the Atlantic Coast Line at the summit, the Southern Railway in the middle, and the Seaboard Air Line lowest. The city lay on a peninsula, and the Havana Special and the other crack Coast Line trains did not deign to come all the way down into town, but only paused briefly at the North Charleston station en route between Florida and New York City.

On Sunday afternoons in the mid-1930s, when we went for automobile drives in the country we sometimes stopped to watch the Havana Special come in. When we first arrived in the parking lot there might be only one or two automobiles outside the station. My sister and brother and I would walk up the tracks beyond the highway viaduct several hundred feet to the north of the station and into a stand of pine trees, or else pull each other around on one of the baggage carts, with their flat-rimmed iron wheels, that lay alongside the tracks.

Gradually the cars in the parking lot became more numerous. There was activity in and about the passenger station with its ivied concrete exterior and overhanging roof. A bus pulled into the parking lot, and the uniformed musicians of the Jenkins Orphanage

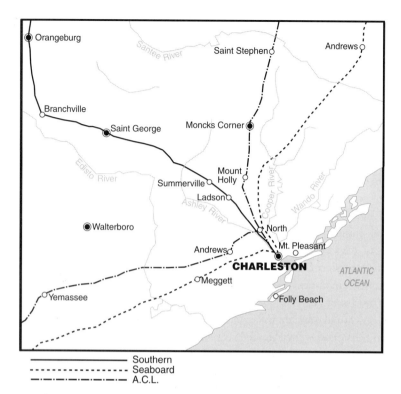

Southern ——————————
Seaboard - - - - - - - -
A.C.L. —·—·—·—·—·—

that one could be sure the train would soon be arriving. Now redcaps with hand trucks stacked with suitcases moved up the trackside to where the Pullmans would stop, followed by the travelers who would be boarding the train.

Far up the right-of-way, where the double sets of tracks converged in a haze at the horizon, was where we looked for the sign of smoke. Was the blur over the space above the roadbed and the low line of trees on either side an indication that the train was soon to appear, or was it no more than a compound of dust and afternoon heat rising from the steel rails? We trained our vision on the spot to make something of what we saw, but there was no change, no development.

Off to the west we could hear the whistle of a locomotive on the Southern tracks, out of sight a mile or more away. But this was the Coast Line, and this was the Havana Special that would soon be arriving from New York City.

There *was* smoke. Definitely so: a smudge that was staining the sky above the tracks. A minute, and then within it, on the horizon, a dot that as it grew larger materialized into a locomotive and a plume of black smoke came toward us, still far up the right-of-way but moving in our direction. Then it became plainly a locomotive, with a headlamp in the center of its cylindrical smoke box, bell above, and the cowcatcher and coupler below, pounding along the rails toward us. As it drew closer we could see that there were not one but two locomotives, a doubleheader, twin 4–6–2 Pacific passenger engines, glossy black, their drive wheels stroking in unison and gray smoke fanning from their stacks, coming powerfully toward where we waited, rolling underneath the viaduct and into the station area.

They were upon and past us, the high drive wheels turning over, white steam hissing from the pistons, the revolving bell overhead clanging, then the broad firebox and cab of the leading locomotive, the fireman gazing down noncommittally as he swung by high above us, and the second locomotive following,

Band got out, an array of black youths bearing assorted horns and drums as they walked up the tracks to position themselves. Soon they began performing, while one youngster, small and with an oversize visored hat, conveyed the beat with his baton, and several others of similar size, with upturned hats extended, moved along the trackside where people were beginning to gather.

Inside the waiting room the telegraph instruments kept up a steady clicking behind the ticket windows, contributing a staccato chatter to what as train time came closer was a building sense of anticipation. The mail clerks commenced to trundle their baggage carts, heaped high with gray asbestos sacks, well along the tracks to where the forward end of the train would be stopping. But it was not until a pair of elongated, dark blue buses of ancient vintage, with leather seats and rows of doors on the sides, rolled into the station from the city, pulled up in front of the ticket office, and began discharging outbound passengers and luggage, equally consequential, the ground beneath our feet vibrating from their force. Then the baggage and mail coaches, and the lead day coaches, and a dining car with fogged galley windows, and a lounge, and more coaches, and another dining car, and then the string of Pullman sleeping cars. Below the coaches the brake shoes were shooting sparks as they bit into the flanged wheels, filling the air with a hot iron smell that tempered the acrid steam, as the 18-coach-long train slowed to a crawl, and finally to a stop. With a hiss of steam the air brakes were eased off, and train No. 75, the southbound Havana Special, double-headed, had arrived at North Charleston, bearing travelers from New York, Philadelphia, Baltimore, Washington, and Richmond.

The Pullman porters opened the vestibule doors and began handing luggage to the redcaps. The iron floors swung up, and the metal stairways dropped into position. Porters leaned out of vestibules, wiped the handrails clean, positioned their yellow footstools, stepped down, and began helping the disembarking passengers onto the ground. "Stand back, please!" they called to the clusters of people who had gathered around the vestibule doors. For the next few minutes there was excitement as inbound travelers were greeted and embraced, hand luggage was claimed, gratuities were bestowed upon the porters, and suitcases were stacked on hand trucks by redcaps.

One after another the arriving passengers and those who had come to greet them moved away toward the station. It was time for the outbound passengers to climb aboard, and those who came to see them off waved goodbye. Women were touching handkerchiefs to their eyes. As the travelers moved into the interior of the cars to find their assigned accommodations, their families and friends walked along the side of the Pullman cars, peering up at the windows, and upon spotting those they were seeing off, stood below to pantomime last-minute reminders and farewells.

A quietness descended upon the station area. Off to one side the Jenkins Band continued to tootle away.

Most of the inbound passengers and their welcomers had left trackside and were now waiting at the baggage master's shed for checked luggage, or else proceeding toward automobiles, taxis, and buses. There were still a few people gathered below the Pullman and day-coach windows, but the porters and trainmen, their responsibilities completed, were waiting around near the vestibules. From the head end the mail clerk, having delivered the outgoing postal sacks, pulled a baggage cart heaped with sacks of incoming mail along the track in the direction of the station.

Standing on the ground outside a vestibule door, the Pullman conductor, pocket watch in hand, was gazing up the tracks. Waving a white card above his head, he signaled toward the head end. Moments later, from the train conductor up ahead came a call: "*Boaaaarrrrrddd!*"

"*All aboard!*" the Pullman conductor shouted in response, and stepped up into the vestibule. The porters retrieved their yellow footstools and climbed up into the train, and there was a series of bangs as the metal floors slammed into place and the doors closed over them.

The coaches drifted back several inches as the air brakes were released, then eased forward decisively. The train began to roll, at first slowly, then more powerfully. Before long the coaches were swinging past us. The last Pullman swept by, and abruptly there was open space over the tracks. We watched down the way as the train moved off, red lanterns mounted alongside the vestibule. Up ahead the twin locomotives now swung into full view, piston rods stroking in unison and black smoke belching from their stacks as they rolled into the wide curve to the west and then disappeared from sight behind a bluff, bound for Savannah and points south with the long train following after.

We walked along the now-quiet trackside and past the ticket office. Inside it the telegraph receivers continued their clicking. The last of the downtown buses was leaving the station. The Jenkins Band bus departed. Only a few automobiles remained in the parking lot. In one of them our parents were waiting for us. We climbed into the back seat of the car, and my father drove homeward.

———

My interest in trains came from my father. He was an electrical contractor and retailer, and he knew the people at the Southern Railway roundhouse in downtown Charleston. On Sunday mornings sometimes he would take my sister and myself there. The trainmen would lead us into the roundhouse, with its turntable that could be swung around to any of the locomotives housed in the semi-circular building. Or we might be boosted up into the cab of a newly arrived locomotive, and perhaps be allowed to ride aboard it as it was moved into its stall. There were iron castings to play with, rusty track spikes, discarded valves and rods. In the process we would get thoroughly grimy in spite of the sets of coveralls we were wearing, made of the same striped gray denim as those worn by the trainmen.

In the holiday season the show window of my father's electrical store was filled with Lionel and American Flyer trains. On Christmas morning he took me to the store and let me work the transformers and move them ahead and in reverse, through the switches and tunnels and signal blocks. Once when he had business in Savannah, a hundred miles down the coast, I went with him up to North Charleston, where we boarded the Havana Special, riding in the Pullman to that city.

On Sunday afternoon family excursions, after we crossed the viaduct and were driving homeward along the King Street Road, I would look out for the late afternoon Southern Railway passenger train that always came racing past Magnolia Crossing and along the tracks, its high silver-painted drive wheels pounding and the whistle of its bright green-colored locomotive shrieking as it roared by. For all its brave performance, it was only the 5:20 local, and it traveled no further than Columbia, 120 miles upstate. It did not even have dining and Pullman cars. The morning outward-bound train, the Carolina Special, likewise with a green-and-silver locomotive at its head, was the one that counted

for something. The Specials had strings of coaches, baggage and mail cars, Pullmans, and a diner, and their route was not limited to South Carolina but extended westward across the mountains to Asheville, Knoxville, and Cincinnati, with sleeping cars that continued on to Chicago.

In the winter of 1931–1932 my father was recovering from surgery, and we lived for several months in the town of Summerville, twenty miles from Charleston. Each weekday morning I walked to school with my friends the Hoge brothers down a sandy, tree-lined street. As we went we could hear a train coming, its high-pitched whistle calling in the distance, then growing louder, while the oncoming locomotive produced an enlarging commotion as it drew near town. We watched for it down a cross street, until two blocks away we caught sight of a blur of green locomotive and stroking wheels, and an express train bolted across the gap and out of sight and the procession of coaches and Pullmans flashed past. Within seconds there was only steam and smoke and settling dust down the street, while with whistle screaming and the flanged coach wheels raising a drumming clatter, the train roared through Summerville, past the station and eastward toward Charleston, without even slowing down.

The Hoge brothers knew the telegraph operator at the Summerville railroad station, and in the afternoons sometimes we would go there, listen to the telegraph receivers clicking away behind the ticket counter, scribble on pads of yellow Western Union telegram blanks, and wait for the evening local to arrive from Charleston. Or they might take me out to the tracks not far from their home, less than a mile from the station, where we could climb up onto the embankment, kneel down, and place an ear against the shiny rail to discover whether we could hear the train coming, for long before the whistle became audible in the distance the ticking sound of steel under stress was transmitted along the rails. We placed copper pennies on the tracks, then retreated down the embankment and across the ditch. Presently the train came swinging along, picking up speed. It boomed past us and up the line. Afterwards we climbed back up the embankment and retrieved our pennies, transformed now into thin bright discs.

The Southern Railway's route through Summerville was where scheduled passenger railroading had begun in the United States. In 1831–1833 the merchants of Charleston, in a vain effort to tap the upcountry cotton export trade that was moving by flatboat down the Savannah River to Savannah, had constructed a rail line to Hamburg, South Carolina, opposite Augusta, Georgia. At the Southern Railway shops in Charleston I had seen the replica of the Best Friend of Charleston, the little steam locomotive that in 1831 had pulled the first string of passenger cars, but had blown up soon after its inaugural run when a train worker, annoyed by the noisy safety valve on the boiler, tied it firmly down.

The Southern system was formed in 1894 when J. P. Morgan bought up and consolidated an assortment of rail lines throughout the South. Its various branches led throughout the region, with more than five thousand miles of trackage. "The Southern Serves the South," its slogan went—to which cynics added, "and it serves it right." The Charleston run was far from its most active segment. By the early 1930s the port of Charleston was moribund, most of its waterfront was idle, and little freight was being hauled between the harbor and the hinterland. The green-and-silver locomotives that I so admired were really old-timers, light 4-6-2 Pacific types with high drive wheels and slender domes, and quite sufficient for pulling the limited consists of the passenger trains operating on the line. The freight locomotives, which were not painted green, were 2-8-2 Mikados of World War I vintage and grimy 2-8-0 Consolidation types that dated back to the 1900s.

The Southern's Charleston shops, which themselves dated back to the pre–Civil War era, were located well downtown, between Meeting and King Streets. Passenger trains operated out of the Union Station, over near the Cooper River waterfront. To enter the train

shed the locomotive and coaches proceeded out along a wye that led across salt marsh to the edge of the river, then backed into the station. Though not possessing the glamour and importance of the Coast Line, they were nonetheless genuine trains, not little gas-electric combine coaches like the Seaboard's Boll Weevil.

One Atlantic Coast Line train, the Palmetto Limited, did use the Union Station. (I interpreted the "Limited" to mean that it was restricted in its importance, not that it made only a limited number of station stops.) It was an accommodation train, with a string of Pullmans and a diner, and was scheduled so as to permit sleeping-car patrons in Savannah and Charleston to arrive in New York City in the morning. Instead of calling at North Charleston like the Havana and Florida Specials, it proceeded all the way down the peninsula, then back ten miles to regain the main line.

Several months before our sojourn in Summerville I rode aboard the Palmetto Limited. It was in 1931; I was not quite eight years old. The previous winter the family had moved to Richmond, where my father had undergone surgery for a brain abscess, and when he was allowed to return to Charleston, though not to resume work, we traveled back in a double bedroom. In the morning, as the Palmetto Special moved through coastal Carolina toward Charleston, the train made its way down the Charleston peninsula, went out onto the wye, and backed slowly into Union Station. When we stepped down onto the platform, there was a large sign with white letters over the iron gateway at the end of the tracks: WELCOME TO CHARLESTON. I assumed that it had been placed there to greet us on our return home.

———

After the Summerville interlude there was another hospital stay for my father in Richmond before we returned home to Charleston for good. Once his recovery was far enough along, the time hung heavy on his hands, for he was not allowed to reopen his electrical business. To keep him occupied my parents borrowed money through one of the New Deal home-owners' programs and built a new home up at the foot of Sans Souci Street near the northwest edge of the city, overlooking the Ashley River. Except for two houses close by, there were only woods, open fields, and marshland within a mile of us. To the south the Seaboard Air Line Railway tracks ran along Hampton Park and the campus of The Citadel, the Military College of South Carolina.

From that time on, the little Boll Weevil gas-electric train became part of my everyday existence. I was eleven years old, and thereafter until I was eighteen and we moved away to Richmond I encountered it constantly. Playing football on the Citadel campus—we always had a team, and we always lost to the Hampton Park Terrace team—I might look up and see the Boll Weevil come ticking past at a moderate pace, en route to or from the station at the edge of the park, a single day coach trailing after it, so lacking in the customary furore of railroading that it scarcely announced its presence ahead of time. Or I might be down along the river's edge just beyond our house, hear a faint rolling sound, and look downstream along the marsh a mile and a half away to see the low shape of the little train moving across the wooden span of the trestle that led over the Ashley River.

When at age twelve I entered high school I walked five blocks along Sans Souci Street to Rutledge Avenue and took the trolley car downtown. Sometimes on the way home after school, when the trolley car reached the intersection of Rutledge and Grove Streets an alarm bell might begin beating and a red warning light pulsing. The guard rails would descend, and after a couple of minutes the southbound Boll Weevil, moving at a very deliberate pace, would clink across Rutledge Avenue, its engine grinding away and its own bell clanging, to pull into the station beyond College Park.

Most memorably, I almost always caught sight of the Boll Weevil while I was seated in the stands at College Park watching Municipal League baseball games. In the 1930s the baseball diamond and the stands were at the southwest corner of College Park, and there was no left-field fence; the outfield stretched all the way to the Seaboard station area and Grove Street. The southbound section usually arrived in midafternoon. Unlike the occasional freight trains, which when they came rumbling past the station and across Rutledge Avenue set up so prodigious a din that the crowd noise was drowned out, when the Boll Weevil put in its appearance—the eastbound near noon-time, the westbound in mid-afternoon—it was done with so little commotion that I almost never actually saw it arrive. At some point during the game I would glance over the expanse of outfield and it would be there, waiting at the pink stucco station which was itself just out of sight behind a mass of oleander bushes along the furthest extension of the left-field foul line. Such Charleston-bound clientele as it had brought with it—never very many—would be departing from the gravel parking lot.

Its departure, customarily after a lengthy wait, was equally without fanfare. The game would absorb my attention, and when later I looked up the Boll Weevil would be gone, having resumed its leisurely journey through the coastal country between Charleston and Savannah, puttering across the railroad bridges that spanned the rivers and creeks and the salt marsh, pausing at the little towns and crossroad stops to drop off mail and baggage and to discharge or take on a passenger or two. Its gas-electric motor car was also baggage coach and railway post office.

Until I was well into my teens my acquaintance with Seaboard Air Line passenger trains was solely with the Boll Weevil, and since it was my custom to judge the relative importance of railroads in terms of their passenger trains, so far as I was concerned the little gas-electric combine typified what I considered to be the Seaboard Air Line's irredeemably inferior status. Later I came to understand that, unlike the Atlantic Coast Line trains that stopped at North Charleston, the Boll Weevils were not the Seaboard's main-line trains, but ran along branch trackage that dipped down from the road's major junction point at Hamlet in a 200-mile-long bow along the seacoast to Charleston and on to Savannah—which happened to be the last significant stretch of new railroad trackage built in South Carolina. The Seaboard's main line lay upstate, with Columbia the midpoint on the line between Savannah and Hamlet. Along that route the Seaboard operated full-fledged passenger trains, too, with steam locomotives, Pullmans, and dining cars. (In railroad parlance the term Air Line originally meant that the trackage went straight across country from one place to another, instead of following along a river valley or a coast.)

I wondered sometimes how the Boll Weevils made their way through the city once they had crossed Rutledge Avenue and were headed uptown and northward. Their route had to lie somewhere west of the Cooper River and east of the King and Meeting Street roads, but just where I did not know.

I thought that I should like to ride the little train up to Hamlet some day, just out of curiosity to see where it went. But the Havana Special and the other name trains on the Atlantic Coast Line were the trains to travel on if one wished to get somewhere. Those were the trains that could take me where I wanted to go.

———

If the Boll Weevil was unobtrusive, not so the Seaboard's freight trains, which came into town across the trestle over the Ashley River, a mile south of our home. In the evenings they could be heard for miles away. For reasons unknown to me all of them seemed to be headed northbound. Never, when lying in bed at night, did I hear a Seaboard freight train bound south toward Savannah. They came from across the river, crossed the trestle, and moved through the uptown city, presumably bound to Hamlet and beyond.

The locomotives pulling the freight trains were long-barreled, with their snouts bedecked with booster tanks, and with the partly rounded Vanderbilt tenders

that the Seaboard favored. In later years, after I learned the steam locomotive classifications, I realized they had been either 2–8–2 Mikados or 4–8–2 Mountain types. Often, with a train of more than ordinary length, they were doubleheaded. In contrast to the freight locomotives on the Atlantic Coast Line, which were always in spic-and-span condition with glossy black paint, those on the Seaboard always seemed dirty and grimy.

It was well known that the Seaboard Air Line was in financial receivership. When I happened to see freight trains at the Rutledge Avenue crossing or while I was watching a baseball game at College Park, I ascribed the heftiness of the steam locomotives to the road's financial straits. Such powerful engines, I thought, must have been meant for more important duties, and were on the Charleston run only because the road lacked a better use for them. Such was the mentality of the Depression Years.

What I did not understand was that the northbound Seaboard freights moving through Charleston at regular intervals, day and night, *were* in fact the road's main-line trains, many of which, unlike the passenger trains, did indeed come through the Charleston branch. The ruling grade along the Charleston branch between Savannah and Hamlet was considerably more favorable for northbound traffic than that on the Savannah-Columbia-Hamlet line. So while the Seaboard's Florida-to-New York passenger trains, and all of its southbound freight traffic, operated through Columbia, it was the road's practice to route its northbound freight trains, and particularly its long red-ball expresses with their strings of refrigerator cars loaded with citrus fruit and produce, via Charleston rather than Columbia, in order to economize on fuel consumption and make better time. So it was not merely my imagination that made it seem that most of the Seaboard freight traffic came through Charleston from the south.

It was at night that I heard them most clearly. In warm weather with the windows open, I lay in my bed and listened to the sounds of the city. I could hear the

Rutledge Avenue trolley car on its run up to Magnolia Crossing and back, uttering a high-pitched whine as it went. There was a launch that came down the Ashley River late each evening, its make-and-break engine identifiable by its steady *putt-putt* as it moved along, very slowly. When to judge from its sound it seemed to be opposite our house out in the ship channel beyond the edge of the marsh a quarter mile or so away, I sometimes tried to watch for it, and occasionally caught sight of a single pinprick of light through the foliage of the water oaks outside the window. Occasionally, too, I could hear the deep-voiced bay of a ship's whistle somewhere out in the harbor downtown.

Mainly, however, what I listened for were the trains. From miles away came faint whistling, which might even be from a Coast Line train as it crossed the river far upstream, though more likely it was a Southern Railway freight moving along the tracks between the King Street and Meeting Street roads north of the city. Somewhere in the yards along the Cooper River beyond Magnolia Cemetery a switch engine was usually at work spotting cars; I could hear the huffing and puffing and the occasional slam of couplers.

But there was another whistle, very faint, a long way off to the west. At first I could not even be certain that I had heard it, until after some minutes it repeated itself. Somewhere across the river, in the western reaches of St. Andrew's Parish, a Seaboard Air Line freight train was moving toward Charleston, blowing for the grade crossings. I tried to imagine how it must have looked in the darkness, its headlamp thrusting its beam of light along the rails, the glow of its firebox reflecting against the pine trees, its drive wheels and pistons working away.

For some time to come the train's whistle was all that could be heard, each time a little more distinct and full-throated when it sounded. Then gradually the noise of the working locomotive itself began to insinuate itself into the discourse, lightly at first but with continuity, a steady rhythm, which as the train drew nearer to the city seemed to divide the night up into a series of drumbeats, growing ever louder until the explosion of the exhaust was reverberating like an artillery barrage. Underneath the throbbing a steady rolling, the drone of steel freight car wheels on rails, became more and more audible as the locomotive drew the train along the embankment leading to the river's edge. When it moved out onto the wooden trestle the pitch turned more hollow, and by the time the locomotive cleared the drawspan and neared the shore there were so many car wheels rolling along the tracks above the river that their clamor filled the darkness.

Then gradually the beat of the exhaust and the pistons began to reassert itself. As more and more cars came off the trestle onto the embankment, the hollow rolling sound diminished in volume. The locomotive and a growing number of boxcars were on solid earth again, booming along the tracks past the campus of The Citadel and next to Hampton Park. The train was moving more slowly, its pace notably slackening as it neared the intersection at Rutledge Avenue. The blast of the exhaust was throttled down into a low chugging, and the other noises of the freight train in motion could be heard. The revolving locomotive bell rang steadily, the freight cars clinked and the chains and couplers rattled, the flanged wheels bumped over the switches, and the crossing alarm was gonging away.

After that came the long retreat of the train, its gradual recession as it cleared the intersection and moved eastward and then northward through Magnolia Crossing and up the peninsula. The sound died down, the sounds of the city reasserted themselves, and the northbound Seaboard freight drag grew indistinguishable from the other night noises. But by then I had fallen asleep.

Five "Life Is Like a Mountain Railroad"

Life is like a mountain railroad,
With an engineer that's brave.
We must make the run successful
From the cradle to the grave.

—Gospel Hymn

Deeply to my disappointment, no job was forth-coming in Charleston. I was told that the paper had expected an increased allotment of newsprint, which was in short supply, but had now learned it was not going to get it. In retrospect my guess is that the authorities, after talking with me, decided that I was not likely to stay on the job for more than a year or so before wanting to move on again. If so, they were probably right, even though I was convinced at the time that Charleston was where I wished to live and work.

I was offered a spot on the morning paper in Columbia, a hundred miles upstate, but at a salary so low that I would never be able to get by on it. So I returned to Richmond. A college friend was working on the afternoon paper in Lynchburg, Virginia, and he arranged an interview for me. There was also an opening in Staunton, in the Shenandoah Valley.

Lynchburg was a considerable railroad crossroads. The Norfolk and Western and the Chesapeake and Ohio Railways, both of which operated coal trains from the mines of Appalachia eastward to Hampton Roads, came through there, as did the Southern Railway's main north-south line from Washington to Atlanta. While in Lynchburg I photographed a 2–6–6–4 Mallet articulated locomotive (<o OOO OOO oo), the first I had ever seen. Designed for heavy-duty work on steep grades, it had a double set of drive wheels, and the pilot truck and forward set of drive wheels could swing independently of the body of the locomotive, allowing it to negotiate curves despite its extended length.

From Lynchburg I took a bus over to Staunton. It was early March, and heavy snow lay over the Blue Ridge Mountains and the Valley. I got off the bus at Staunton, went looking for the newspaper office, and found it down the street in an old building with a plate-glass show window, like a store. I talked with the publisher, a retired National Guard major general, and was offered a job as city editor of the *Staunton News-Leader*, circulation 7,500. The salary was $50 a week—$12 more than I had been earning in New Jersey. No word had arrived from Lynchburg, so I accepted the position.

NORFOLK AND WESTERN RAILWAY

———

On a day in early March 1947, from the window of a day coach on Chesapeake and Ohio train No. 5, the Sportsman, I watched the undulating foothills of Piedmont Virginia go by. The coach had reclining chairs, with single seats on one side of the aisle, and was more roomy and comfortable than any I had ever encountered before. At the head end was a powerful 4–8–4 steam locomotive, known as a Northern on

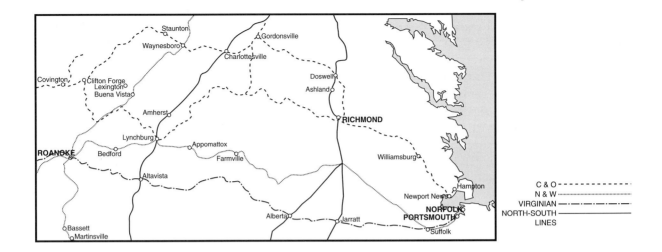

C & O	- - - - - - -
N & W	··············
VIRGINIAN	—·—·—·—
NORTH-SOUTH LINES	——————

most railroads but on the C&O referred to as a Greenbrier. West of Charlottesville the train headed for the Afton Mountain tunnel through the Blue Ridge. Beyond lay Waynesboro, and after it Staunton.

Staunton was on the C&O's Mountain Division. Between Richmond and Clifton Forge, Virginia, fifty miles farther west of Staunton, the C&O operated two separate divisions. The coal traffic moved eastward along the more advantageous grades of the James River plain, which crossed the Blue Ridge some fifty miles to the south of Staunton and led through Lynchburg. The passenger trains and the manifest freight runs came through Staunton, on the Mountain Division. The Sportsman and the C&O's major name train, the George Washington, operated in two sections, one from Newport News via Richmond, the other from Washington, D.C. At Charlottesville they combined for the westward run, although sometimes both sections continued as separate trains. Another through train, the FFV—the Fast Flying Virginian—also operated westward in two sections that joined in Charlottesville for the westbound run, but without a Richmond-Newport News section eastbound. Several local passenger trains also came through Staunton.

I worked on the newspaper six nights a week, finishing up after the first and only edition came off the presses sometime after one A.M. It was a very small operation with only a single reporter. No Monday morning paper was published, which meant that after the paper appeared on Sunday morning I was free until late Monday afternoon.

It did not take me long to begin exploring the railroad opportunities. This was my first experience of mountain railroading, and the steam locomotives employed to handle the steep grades of the southern Blue Ridge and the Alleghenies were larger and more powerful than any I had previously seen at work. The Chesapeake and Ohio Railway was one of three major railroads hauling bituminous coal across the state of Virginia down to the Chesapeake Bay, where the ships waited that would bear it all over the world. Several hundred million tons of coals each year were loaded into hopper cars at the mines of southwestern Virginia, West Virginia, and eastern Kentucky, taken down to classification yards for sorting, then shipped to the tidewater for export. The C&O and its arch-rival Norfolk and Western were the largest coal carriers in the nation. The Virginian Railway also carried a considerable share of the traffic. As coal-hauling roads, all three declined to have anything to do with diesel-electric power. They earned their money carrying bituminous coal, and unlike other coal-carrying roads such as the

Baltimore and Ohio up in Maryland, they meant to stick with and by it for their own trains.

There was a local train westbound to Clifton Forge, where the Mountain and James River Division lines were united and C&O's extensive locomotive and car repair shops were located. On a Sunday morning I rode to Clifton Forge and spent the afternoon photographing an array of large and powerful locomotives, in particular the C&O's 2–6–6–6 H-8 Alleghenies, enormous articulated Mallets specifically designed to move long trains of coal over the mountains. With their double sets of drive wheels, fronts stacked with pumps, extended pilot trucks with the headlamp mounted down on the truck, and large pipes above the pistons and wheels, they were an awesome sight. I photographed them as they were turned at the roundhouse, as they were standing in the yards waiting to take up assignments, and at the head of trains of loaded hopper cars leaving for the James River Division or pulling empties back across the Alleghenies to be filled with more coal. The H-8s were all of recent manufacture, and they looked it. They were magnificent machines.

Very much present, too, were the 4–8–4 Greenbriers and the 2–8–4 Kanawhas, powerful engines in their own right, and in size, weight, and tractive effort surpassing any of the locomotives I had encountered up in northern New Jersey. There were also some older 4–8–2's, 2–8–2 Mikados, 4–6–2 Pacifics, and assorted yard engines. The roundhouse full of these locomotives, with a mountainside for a backdrop, was a sight to behold.

After walking around the yards and the roundhouse, I installed myself on a bench alongside the tracks at the passenger station, a large rambling wooden structure that was connected to a railroad YMCA, and spent the remainder of the afternoon watching steam locomotives and strings of hopper cars and box cars lumber by, their axles churning and their chains rattling and clinking, with 0–8–0 switch engines moving cars about and occasionally a coal train arriving or departing. That evening I took a Sunday-only local back to Staunton,

riding in an old but well-maintained coach. The train was almost deserted; in its three coaches there were not a half-dozen passengers.

———

On another Sunday I rode a bus to Roanoke, eighty miles down—or, since the Valley ran south to north, up the valley. Not far from Roanoke the bus stopped in front of a college campus, with red brick buildings set back in the trees. I had no way of knowing how importantly it was to figure in my life a decade later. At Roanoke I headed for the Union Station and located myself at a point where the tracks divided, near the shops at Shaffers Crossing.

The Norfolk and Western's main line ran between Hampton Roads and western Virginia, from where trunk lines led northwest across West Virginia to Cincinnati and southwest to a connection with the Southern Railway at Bristol. Another line led due south to Winston-Salem, North Carolina, along a right-of-way so winding that it was known as the Pumpkin Vine. Still another, the Shenandoah Division, ran northward through the Valley, crossing the C&O at several points and continuing on to Hagerstown, Maryland, where it connected with the Pennsylvania Railroad. All these lines came together at a junction in Roanoke not far from where I stood waiting with my camera.

The N&W was unusual among railroads in that it did not purchase its motive power from any of the several manufacturers of locomotives, but built its own, specifically designed for mountain railroading, in Roanoke. As a major hauler of coal, it had no intention of conceding anything to the diesels; instead it set out to build steam locomotives that were capable of competing with them. I was not at the station for very long before a Y-class 2–8–8–2 Mallet came rumbling along the main line at the head of a long string of loaded hopper cars. It was a compound articulated locomotive—which is to say, it used steam twice, once in each set of pistons to power its double sets of drive wheels. With a huge firebox, roller bearings, and pressure lubrication, it could operate over long stretches of track before needing to have its firebox cleaned of ashes. Moreover, the N&W's engine houses could service a Y-class locomotive within an hour's time.

A westbound passenger train, the Powhatan Arrow, rolled in from Norfolk. Its locomotive, encased in a handsome black-and-red streamlined jacket, was a J-class 4–8–4. For a passenger locomotive it had relatively small drive wheels, but it could move a train along a straight stretch of tracks at more than a hundred miles an hour, and on mountain grades exert great tractive strength. Other locomotives put in their appearance, too—several varieties of Mallets, including 2–6–6–4's and older 2–6–6–2's, as well as a 4–8–2 passenger locomotive. There were even some 0–8–0 switch engines of very recent manufacture.

I took a taxi over to the Virginian yards, located a mile to the south. The Virginian Railway had an interesting history. Unlike most Southern railroads, it did not emerge as the result of consolidation of assorted shorter segments by Northern holding companies during the later nineteenth century. Instead it was conceived and built almost totally as a unit early in the twentieth century by Henry Huddleston Rogers, one of John D. Rockefeller's associates at Standard Oil Company and a close friend and companion of Mark Twain. Rogers conceived and developed the railroad for one use only: to haul coal from the mountains to the sea. The route was surveyed and constructed without regard for any cities and towns en route; the right-of-way was located where it would be as free of uphill grades and as close to forming a straight line as was feasible in hilly terrain. Rogers spent $50,000,000 to build it, and when it opened for business in 1909 Mark Twain was among those who came along for the inaugural run.

The Virginian operated a few local passenger and freight trains, but the coal traffic was what mattered. It was the only major Class I railroad on which passenger trains regularly took to the sidings and waited for the freight trains to come through. West of Roanoke a 134-mile stretch of the road was electrified. From Roanoke to the tidewater coal was moved down in long trains powered by Mallet locomotives, including some 2–6–6–6's that I was told were a bit more powerful even than those purchased by the C&O from Lima Locomotive Works. I photographed several of them, as well as some of the powerful box-cab electric locomotives that brought coal trains in from the west.

For the return trip to Staunton I boarded an N&W passenger train powered by a J-class 4–8–4, enjoyed an excellent meal in a dining car as it headed northward, and got off in Waynesboro. There I climbed the station stairs up to the upper level and waited for the westbound George Washington, powered by a pair of 2–8–4 Kanawhas, which hauled me the remaining thirteen miles to Staunton. In the course of a single day I had ridden aboard trains of two coal-hauling Virginia railroads and spent several hours observing and taking photographs of a third. I had viewed some of the most powerful steam locomotives in existence.

———

It was well that I could find occasional trips to take on Sundays to watch trains, because when not involved in the routine of my newspaper job, there was little else to my life that I found very satisfactory. I had no friends, male or female, in Staunton, and working the hours that I did, was without opportunity to meet anyone other than employees of the newspaper. At age 23 I lived a solitary life.

I began work in the late afternoon, and except for an hour to eat dinner at a nearby restaurant, stayed on the job until the first edition came off the press in the early morning hours. After checking the front page I went by an all-night restaurant for supper, then to my room, where I read until I grew sleepy. When I awoke it was close to midday, and I dressed and walked to a restaurant for breakfast at about the time that most people were eating lunch. After that I went by the newspaper office to see what mail I might have received.

Some afternoons I walked two blocks over to the railroad station. The Sportsman arrived in mid-afternoon, and I could watch that. Freight trains also came through occasionally. One afternoon the pilot truck wheel of a freight locomotive jumped the track, and I followed what happened until it was back on the rails, then wrote a feature story about it. A short-line freight railroad running from Harrisonburg to Staunton, the Chesapeake Western, brought a few freight cars over for interchange each day, pulled by a road switcher diesel, and I walked out along its right-of-way and photographed it.

—

When I finished up sometime after one in the morning, if the weather was good, after eating supper in the all-night restaurant I would sometimes go over to the C&O station. The station was located alongside a cliff, with the tracks and the columned train shed curving in a wide arc around its steep rock face. Usually I went out beyond the station building to the end of the platform, where there were always a few baggage carts around to find a seat on. An eastbound freight train always came through town a little before two A.M. I waited to hear it blowing for crossings out to the west. It reminded me of the way the Seaboard freights used to come into Charleston from across the river when I was a child. From first hearing until the locomotive headlamp materialized from around a curve, however, took much less time than I remembered the northbound Seaboard freights taking to arrive in Charleston from out across the river, whether because in hilly terrain the whistle sounds could not be heard from nearly as far away, or because the trains were simply running faster, I could not say.

The two A.M. freight was usually pulled by a pair of 4–8–2 Mountain locomotives, and as it moved into the station area itself the headlamp of the lead locomotive brought into momentary view numerous objects I had not hitherto made out: semaphores, switch blocks, boxcars on a siding, a warehouse alongside the tracks,

a cattle-loading corral and ramp. The beam played upon the jagged rock walk of the cliffside, breaking it into a mosaic of planes and recesses. The locomotives churned powerfully up and past, their drive wheels performing in unison, and for a moment I could see the engine crews in their cabs, high above the tracks. The freight cars came rattling along in the dark, one after another, the drone of their wheels punctuated by a medley of creaks, bangs, and bumps, eighty cars or more, until the caboose swung by and swiftly out of sight around the bend.

One evening in mid-spring the night air was so balmy that I not only stayed to watch the night freight, but sat on for a while after it had passed, listening to its whistle receding eastward toward Waynesboro and the Blue Ridge Mountains beyond. Then all was quiet except for an occasional trailer-truck in low gear climbing the hill on U.S. Highway 11 several blocks east of the station. It was so pleasant that I did not want to leave for my room. So I stayed put.

After a time I realized that the faint whistling in the east was no longer that of the receding night freight, but another train, coming westward. It was now well after three A.M. I decided that the westbound train must be the FFV, a passenger train that I had never actually seen. I listened as it rolled toward town, ever more loudly, until the night was ringing with the noise of its coming. A man and a woman were awaiting its arrival, standing in front of the station. A clerk came along the platform, pulling a cart with mail sacks and packages, and took up position beyond where I was sitting. This was the train, I knew, onto which bundles of the newspaper I had edited earlier that evening would be loaded to be dropped off at Millboro, forty miles west of the city.

No matter how many times I might have watched trains pulling into stations, the arrival of another one was always exciting. The locomotive came gliding in from around the bend, its headlight bending the shadows of the platform's columned arcade. A 4–8–4, it barged past me and eased to a stop a hundred yards up the track, the steam hissing from its valves. Even at that hour there were passengers debarking. The man and woman I had seen waiting were apparently the only outbound travelers. They stepped aboard, the Pullman porter following with their luggage. The mail clerk worked away at handing up the asbestos bags of newspapers to someone in the mail car. The conductor and brakeman walked along toward the rear of the train.

After a time I heard the conductor calling *"All aboard!"* and saw him signaling with his flashlight to the engineer. The locomotive coughed twice, and the train began to ease forward. The darkened coaches moved by, then a dining car, looking cold and dark. The train rapidly gained speed. The Pullman sleepers swung past last, their names—Gauley Bridge, City of Ashland, Balcony Falls, and so on—briefly in view as they swept past. It was a long train, bound for Cincinnati and the Midwest, where I had never been. I watched until the red lanterns on the rear vestibule receded westward and out of sight. Soon the whistle was blowing for crossings and the locomotive was stroking powerfully along the rising grade toward Clifton Forge and the Alleghenies. It was after four A.M. when I got back to my room.

———

There was excitement on the Chesapeake and Ohio Railways in those years. The war was over, gasoline rationing had ended, and new automobiles were becoming available. Trains were no longer crowded with travelers. Even so, and in the face of the nationwide falling-off of passenger traffic, the chairman of the board of the C&O, Robert R. Young, embarked upon a full-scale campaign to prove the continuing viability of railroad passenger service. It was Young's belief that the American railroads were controlled by conservative banker combinations and unimaginative administrators, more concerned with protecting their own bailiwicks than in seeking ways to improve and enhance service and to attract new riders. Fastening upon the fact that it was impossible for railroad

passengers to travel across the United States without changing trains and stations in Chicago, he ran full-page advertisements in magazines and newspapers. "A Hog Can Travel Across the Country Without Changing Trains," they proclaimed, "—But YOU Can't!" Pullman cars, he declared, were "rolling tenements."

He withdrew the C&O from membership in the Association of American Railroads, which he considered a sluggish, moribund affair, and founded the Federation for Railway Progress. He instituted credit cards for purchasing tickets while on board trains—this was long before the day of general-use credit cards. He set up a central reservations bureau, and he supplemented the road's conductors with hostesses and passenger representatives. The C&O even announced a no-tipping policy for dining car waiters and porters; such gratuities, Young declared, were un-American and demeaning. In the tables of dining cars on C&O trains appeared signs stating the policy and assuring passengers that the car's waiters had been adequately recompensed for the loss of revenue thereby.

Not long after the no-gratuity rule went into effect, I ate lunch aboard the Sportsman en route from Richmond to Staunton. When time came to pay the bill, the waiter stood by the table, waiting. I felt awkward. "Are we supposed not to leave a tip?" I asked.

"That's what it says," the waiter responded dolefully.

I left one anyway. After several months the signs disappeared from the dining-car tables, and normal tipping procedure was once again followed in theory as well as practice. It was a noble try, but Young was up against too many decades of accumulated travel customs.

Young's ideas and his tactics were well publicized, and they aroused resentment among the railroad moguls. On one occasion he announced that he was going to simplify the way of presenting timetables, which he maintained were needlessly difficult to read. He introduced a timetable consisting of a cardboard rectangle with disks at each end. There were little slots in the disks next to the names of stations, and what the user did was to turn one disk to the desired place of departure and one to the destination. The slots would reveal the times that the trains departed and arrived.

A newspaper reporter in Richmond called the president of the Southern Railway and asked whether his road intended to follow the C&O's lead. "Humph!" the Southern president snorted. "He can do that; he's only got three through trains on his road. We couldn't get all of ours on a disk without making it the size of a manhole cover!"

Young also spent large sums of money to eliminate bends and turns in the line and to reduce steep grades by excavating cuts, building new bridges and filling in declivities. He ordered lightweight equipment for a new all-coach supertrain, to be called the Chessie, which when inaugurated would provide new twelve-hour daylight service between Washington and Cincinnati.

His most ambitious innovation was a steam-turbine locomotive that was designed to save the day for coal-powered steam. A five-tube boiler was mounted behind the cab, and a coal bunker was installed in the locomotive's streamlined nose. Like the diesels, the drive wheels were propelled by an electric traction engine, which, however, received its power from a turbine driven by the boiler's steam instead of from an oil-burning diesel engine. Three of the locomotives were built, numbered 500, 501 and 502. Much attention was trained upon them, for if they proved successful, the possibility existed that the decline of steam locomotion could well be reversed and the seemingly inexorable progress of dieselization halted. Road tests showed that the locomotives could exert tremendous power and handle long trains at high speeds.

The first of the locomotives, the 500, was sent upon a triumphal tour of the C&O's main line. Crowds turned out for its announced arrival at the various stations along the route. For my newspaper it was big news. I headlined it prominently.

On the afternoon of the 500's arrival I photographed it as it came rolling across the trestle over U.S. Highway 11 and into the station. It was very

long, with a streamlined, shiny, stainless-steel body. Unlike conventional steam locomotives its exhaust emitted no *chug-chug-chug,* and there were no pistons exploding and clouds of white steam escaping. Instead, its power plant gave out a loud howl, like a banshee keening in an unvaried monotone. Still, a plume of black coal smoke did curl from an out-of-sight stack.

There was a long-retired engineer of the C&O, Mr. Ben Snapp, who lived in a rooming house not far from the railroad station. He was in his eighties and had first gone to work for the C&O shortly after the turn of the century. I had arranged with the old engineer's son to bring his father by the station so that he could go aboard the locomotive cab. The old gentleman mounted the ladder and stepped into the cab; the 500's engineer recognized him at once and escorted him over to the engineer's seat. Tall with flowing white moustaches and a wide-brimmed straw hat, and smoking his pipe, he made himself right at home. To the delight of all the railwaymen present he grasped the locomotive throttle and leaned out of the cab window as if sighting down the tracks.

Afterward the 500 and its train of streamlined coaches departed for Clifton Forge, and thereafter no more was reported from or about it. Several months afterward, in the early hours one morning while I was in my room reading, I heard it, or one of its counterparts, come into Staunton, probably at the head of the FFV. It was summer, windows were open all over Staunton, and the sound was unmistakable and unremitting. It made a fuss like no other locomotive. Not again did I ever see or hear one. In 1950 all three locomotives were sold for scrap.

I have been told that the steam turbines that were designed to stave off the diesels turned out to consume prodigious quantities of powdered coal. I have also read that that was not the problem. According to the railroad historian Thomas W. Dixon, Jr., they actually performed their jobs well, but too often they broke down: "They were one-of-a-kind of an entirely new technology, and no one out on the road was trained or ready to maintain them, nor was the right equipment available." A similar project on the Norfolk and Western also failed to work out. In any event, to the disappointment of steam locomotive devotees, the dieselization of American railroads proceeded apace.

The attitude of most railroad buffs, myself included, toward diesel-electrics was ambivalent. Now that the war was done and new equipment was obtainable, the diesel-electrics were multiplying on railroads everywhere. On the one hand, we wanted very much for the railroads to prosper; we wanted passenger service to thrive. We recognized that the diesels were more efficient, that they consumed less fuel and required less maintenance. A steam locomotive, a railroad man once told me, could pull anything it could start; a diesel could start anything it could pull.

Yet the interest and affection of most of us was for the doomed steam locomotives. So we kept hoping that they would be able somehow to hold their own. In point of fact, even if the steam-turbine power had turned out to be practical, from the standpoint of watching and photographing they would still have been only marginally more interesting than the diesels. Except for the plume of coal smoke, they were not very picturesque. There were no exposed drive wheels, no piston rods stroking away, no explosions of sound and steam. The working machinery was covered up, like the diesel-electrics, not located on the outside and in plain view.

As for railroad passenger service, diesels or not the decline continued. The C&O was turning a decent profit, but on its coal-carrying operations, not its passenger trains. Despite all that Robert R. Young could do, fewer people rode his and other passenger trains each year. Ultimately he faced up to it. Plans for the new all-coach Chessie, which the steam-turbine locomotives were designed to pull, were canceled before the train ever took to the rails. Eventually Young transferred his control and his attentions to the New York Central Railroad, and the C&O no longer positioned itself in the vanguard of what was ultimately a lost cause. For a period of years, however, including those when I was working in Staunton, Young put up a splendid fight, and I was privileged to be able to watch it from up close.

———

What I remember most vividly of all about Young's valiant effort to make the C&O's passenger service more attractive to the riding public was something that took place on a cold early Sunday morning in late winter, not long after I had first come to Staunton. I had checked the first copy of the paper to come off the press, stopped at the all-night restaurant for supper, then gone back to my room. I read awhile, then tried to go to sleep, but was I unable to do so. It was getting on toward daybreak, and I decided to dress, go over to the station, and take the George Washington home to Richmond.

The night air was penetratingly cold, and there was snow everywhere. Tired, shivering, I waited for the train to arrive from the west. At length the double-headed 2–8–4's came into the station at the head of the long train, and I went aboard a coach. I placed my suitcase on a seat and walked back to wait for the dining car's scheduled opening. Others were already in line. I was still chilled from my vigil on the train platform.

Not long after the George Washington left Staunton the doors to the double-coach dining car opened. Before the waiters began taking orders they walked along the tables and poured out steaming demitasse cups of thick black railroad coffee for all present. Sipping it, watching through the fogged windows as the train moved across the snowy Blue Ridge, I was very grateful. It was a small thing, a creature comfort I have never forgotten.

Six Excursions

The drivers were rapidly pounding
While the engine was trembling with steam
—song, "The Wreck of the Sportsman"

Except for the occasional expeditions to places where there were trains to photograph, when I was not on the job at the newspaper the time hung heavy on my hands. At age 24, working six evenings a week from late afternoon until one A.M., I was without any opportunity to meet others my own age, female or male. Sundays were the dreariest days. I would sleep until late morning, then get up and walk downtown for breakfast at a restaurant, while all around me were people going to and from church. I would buy copies of the Sunday *New York Times* and the *Richmond Times-Dispatch*, return to my room after breakfast to read them, and wait for the three P.M. Philharmonic radio broadcast. I ought to be writing, I told myself, but there was nothing I could write or wanted to write about, and of course no one to talk with about writing and books. There was a college campus just around the corner, but I neither knew nor had occasion to meet anyone either on the faculty or in the student body.

When time came for dinner I went out again, then either back to my room to read or else down to the station to see the two sections of the George Washington come through. I watched the trains arrive, discharge and take on passengers, and leave for the Midwest—for Cincinnati, Indianapolis, Chicago, places I had never been. I had read, in Carl Sandburg's poems and elsewhere, of high-speed railroad trains streaking across the prairie, and wanted to see them and ride on them. But all I could do was to look on as the receding lanterns on the George Washington's

rear observation car headed for the mountains of West Virginia.

I could take a bus to Richmond on Sunday mornings and return on the Sportsman Monday afternoon, but most of my friends from my college years, male and female, were now married, or had moved away, or both.

I was always glad when Sunday evening was over. On Monday I would be able to go to work.

———

I decided to buy an automobile. The war had been over for less than two years, and almost all used cars were of pre-Pearl Harbor vintage, and expensive. I ended up buying an eleven-year-old Plymouth coupe, paying $400 for it—or about one-fourth of what a new car would have cost if any had been available, which they were not, nor could I have afforded one if they had been. As it was, I borrowed the money from a local bank, with my father endorsing the note. It was not much of a car. Within a year's time I ended up having to have a rebuilt engine block installed. But it was my first, and it meant that railroad centers that were three or four hours distant from Staunton and difficult or impossible of access by train or bus were now open for exploration.

I drove across the Blue Ridge to Charlottesville and southward along the main line of the Southern Railway, paralleling U.S. Highway 29, taking photographs on the way. I visited the Southern shops at Monroe, well known in song as the place from which

"Old 97, the fastest mail train / That ran on the Southern line," set out for its ill-fated wreck on the "mighty rough road from Lynchburg to Danville." The Southern was using Electro-Motive road diesel locomotives on many of its through trains, but there were still some steam locomotives on the roster and hauling freight. I photographed a handsome 2–8–2 Mikado at Monroe, and another pulling a way freight.

I made another visit to Roanoke, photographing more trains on the Norfolk and Western and the Virginian. At Waynesboro I photographed a J-class N&W 4–8–4 standing in the station at the head of a passenger train, with the coaches of the C&O Sportsman above it on the upper-level tracks. In Richmond I visited the various railroad yards, including the C&O's Fulton Yards where the coal trains were sorted out for the final leg of the journey to Chesapeake Bay.

My most ambitious railroad foray was made on a weekend in January 1948. I wanted to see and photograph trains on the Baltimore and Ohio Railway, which like the C&O, the N&W, and the Virginian hauled coal from the West Virginia mountains to Chesapeake Bay. Early Sunday morning, after I finished up work, I drove 125 miles down the Shenandoah Valley to Winchester, Virginia, where I checked into a hotel at about four A.M. It was after midday before I set out for Martinsburg, where the B&O east-west main line traversed the West Virginia panhandle.

The afternoon was cold and gray, with low-lying clouds. At Martinsburg I photographed a locomotive of a type that I had not previously encountered, a 2–10–2 (<o OOOOO o), known as a Santa Fe. I knew that the B&O operated 2–8–8–4 Mallet locomotives and I hoped to photograph one of those, but none was in evidence. I decided to follow the main line westward, along a road that approximately paralleled the tracks. It was not yet four P.M., but the sky was darkening, and as I drove into the mountains light snow lay on the ground.

Across the West Virginia state line in Maryland, the B&O trackage, which paralleled the course of the Potomac River, followed a long curve around a steep hillside into the town of Hancock. I should have liked to go on another forty miles to Cumberland, where the B&O's main line divided, with one arm extending up to Pittsburgh and across the upper Midwest to Chicago, while the other continued on to Cincinnati and across the lower Midwest to St. Louis. But it was getting late and I was afraid to drive any further westward into the high mountains, where I might well encounter falling snow. So I pulled into the station parking lot at Hancock and decided to wait there to see what might develop.

Unlike the Virginia coal-carrying roads, for whom coal traffic constituted almost four-fifths of their revenue, the B&O did a substantial business in general freight, and it operated numerous passenger trains. Because its dependence upon coal-hauling was less urgent, the road was putting up no all-out resistance to the coming of the diesels, and there were already a number of road and yard diesels on its roster. So I was not surprised when a passenger train with two Electro-Motive road units, silver and dark blue, came snaking around the hillside, bound for Washington and Baltimore.

Silhouetted against the dusting of snow that lay between the tracks and over the hillside and surrounding area, the train made a vivid, if somewhat sinister, appearance. In the murky afternoon under the low cloud cover the lead locomotive's headlamp shone brightly as it sped through the station area. I photographed it and watched it drone eastward below a tier of block signals.

By then it was after 4:30 in the afternoon. Little light was left in the overcast January sky, and what remained was receding. Even if a coal train powered by a pair of the B&O's big 2–8–8–4s were to happen along, I would have to shoot at a shutter speed so slow that the image of the moving locomotives would be blurred. I decided to call it quits and renew my quest the next day. Washington was a couple of hours to the east; I would drive there, check into a hotel, and in the morning return to a point along the line where the B&O's Baltimore and Washington lines joined, photograph trains for a couple of hours, then head back up the Valley to Staunton in time to go to work Monday afternoon. I had no particular reason to go to Washington; I merely wanted to be able to say that I had driven there in my own car.

At Gaithersburg, Maryland, twenty miles out, I topped a viaduct to find an automobile and a dump truck halted on the far slope. I tried to steer between them, but my car struck the automobile a glancing blow. The dump truck crew had been sprinkling ashes on the icy slope of the viaduct to forestall skids, and the driver of the car blocking the road was the district highway supervisor. The viaduct was over the main line of the B&O Railroad.

The next morning, my recently acquired automobile now disfigured by a bent fender and a stove-in headlight, I drove back to Staunton.

———

Purchase of the car had brought an unexpected railroad dividend. Ten miles from Staunton was a preparatory school, and, although it was not my duty to do so, I drove out regularly to cover its football team's practices and home games. The team finished the season undefeated and was chosen to play a prep school bowl game in Chattanooga, and the coach invited me to go along on the bus, all expenses paid. Chattanooga was on the far side of the southern mountains, where I had never been. It was not exactly the Midwestern prairie, but there would be several new railroads for me to photograph. We left on a chartered bus on a Friday morning, arriving in Knoxville in time for the team to work out at the University of Tennessee and for me to head for the Louisville and Nashville Railway yards, where I photographed a 2–8–2 and a 2–8–0 freight locomotive. Tucked alongside an embankment near the edge of the campus were several coaches, a few boxcars, and an antique and small but well-groomed 4–6–2, belonging to the Smoky Mountain Railroad,

a 30-mile short line running up to Sevierville in the western foothills of the Appalachians.

In Chattanooga I saw an even older locomotive, the General, the ancient 4–4–0 wood-burner that had figured in the great locomotive chase during the Civil War and was now on display inside the Chattanooga Terminal Station. I also went out beyond the platforms at the Union Station and photographed the L&N-Nashville, Chattanooga and St. Louis Railway streamlined train, the Georgian, as it departed for Atlanta with a single Electro-Motive diesel at the head end. A handsome NC&StL 2–8–2 also came steaming past at the head of a freight train, throwing up a mighty cloud of smoke.

Chattanooga was a very smoky place, with numerous ironworks. Later I found my way onto a viaduct overlooking the extensive Southern Railway yards in Chattanooga. Most of the Southern's yard engines and road freight locomotives were still steam-powered, and not far from where I stood a switch engine was throwing up a prodigious quantity of black smoke, while further up the way a mile-wide belt of thick, gray man-made cloud lay over all, blotting from view the far end of the yards and everything beyond.

Recently I revisited the scene. The yard and tracks were still there, but diesels had long since replaced the steam locomotives, and the once-busy foundries were mostly gone. The air was clear, and I could see the towers of downtown Chattanooga without any trouble.

———

One of my jobs on the *Staunton News-Leader* was to serve as stringer for the Richmond bureau of the Associated Press, calling in local stories that seemed worthy of wider circulation. In May of 1948 a vacancy came open on the staff of the Richmond bureau. By then I had learned just about all that there was to getting out a very small daily newspaper, and there was no prospect of advancement, for the managing editor, a man in his fifties, was also the editor of the afternoon paper, which had no managing editor. For as long as I stayed there I would presumably be working six evenings a week, with no more likelihood than ever of meeting any girls.

When I was a youth, to be a staff writer on the AP had always seemed to me to be at the pinnacle of newspaper work. Here was my chance to be that, even though it did involve a one-third cut in pay. The Richmond bureau chief, taking advantage of what obviously was my wish to come to work for him, told me that the American Newspaper Guild prescribed a particular salary. Later I learned that it was a flat-out lie; the AP's contract with the Guild called only for a minimum salary, not a maximum. But I was too eager, and too naive to recognize the deception.

So I moved to Richmond and reported for duty. I had expected to continue doing desk work, since the Richmond bureau's principal task was to collect news from the various affiliated AP newspapers in the state and pass it back and forth. I assumed, however, that I would also be sent out from time to time to report and write stories. Instead, from six P.M. until two A.M. five evenings a week I sat at a typewriter, taking stories over the telephone from correspondents at other state newspapers, rewriting the carbons of stories written for the morning Richmond paper, then rewriting my own rewrites for the early editions of the next day's afternoon newspapers. In exchange for the isolation of a small daily newspaper in the mountains I had substituted the tedium of rewriting other people's prose in a second-line Associated Press bureau.

I had come there because I wanted to *write*. It was writing that had drawn me to newspaper work. I was prepared to perform other tasks, provided that I could do writing as well. But now I found that except for occasional assignments, almost all the writing, as distinguished from rewriting, was done by one man, who had been with the bureau for years and would almost certainly remain there for years to come. And not within living memory had any member of the staff ever been transferred to Washington, or New York, or Chicago, or any of the major AP bureaus. So much for my

youthful romantic notions of what it meant to be an Associated Press staff writer.

———

In sheer desperation I decided to develop a feature about the Chesapeake and Ohio's coal-hauling operations from Richmond to Hampton Roads, to be written on my days off. On a Sunday evening in July I drove over to the C&O's Fulton Yards, near the James River southeast of downtown Richmond, where the coal trains came down from Clifton Forge over the James River Division, paralleling the river and the old C&O canal.

At Fulton Yards the hopper cars were sorted out and most of them dispatched seventy-five miles eastward to the C&O's terminal at Newport News. Except for one key stretch just east of the yards, the run was mostly downhill, and the powerful Mallet 2–6–6–6s which brought coal trains down from the mountains were not needed. The hardest part of the job was to get the coal trains started over the hill. Once beyond it they could continue without difficulty. So the C&O maintained a single older Mallet locomotive at Fulton Yards for use as a pusher to help get the train moving. It was to the Mallet, waiting in position behind the caboose of a coal train, that I was taken that evening.

At the head end, more than a mile along the line and partway up the slope, were doubleheaded 4–8–4s. The arrangement was for the 4–8–4s to release the air brakes and those of the hopper cars, so that they began to drift backward down the slope. There was space between the couplers of each car, which when the cars were fully extended amounted to several car lengths.

The trick was for the Mallet to wait until the strategic instant when the cars had fully telescoped into each other, then apply all its forward power. This would have the effect of shooting the hopper cars forward along the tracks, with the impulse being transmitted from car to car, so that by the time the motion reached the head end, the doubleheaded 4–8–4s would be shoved ahead two car lengths. At that instant they were to apply their power, and the hope was that the resulting momentum would get the long train moving up the grade.

When everything was ready, the lead locomotive signaled with its whistle that the air brakes were going off. Well up the way a series of reports could be heard as the hopper cars began one after the other to drop back against the couplers of those behind them. The *clang! clang! clang!* came nearer, grew louder. Then, just as the weight of the cars was telescoped upon the caboose, the engineer of the Mallet opened the locomotive full throttle. With a roar of the pistons the locomotive lurched forward, sending a staccato progression of coupler blasts toward the head of the train as the coal cars were propelled ahead one after the other.

The road locomotives up forward waited until the shock of the movement shoved them ahead, whereupon their own drive wheels bit into the steel rails in an effort to gain traction.

The train could not sustain its momentum. The Mallet's drive wheels began slipping, and forward motion ceased.

Another try was in order. The locomotive crews made their preparations, and the whole process was repeated—the relaxing of the air brakes, the train drifting back, the Mallet giving it full throttle, the mile-long string of hopper cars shooting forward, the road locomotives striving to pick up the train and keep it moving. Again it could not be sustained. A third attempt produced the same result. Each time there was the same tremendous cacophony, with the couplers slamming into each other, the Mallet locomotive's exhaust exploding and pistons blasting, the steam hissing, then the spluttering of the exhaust and the spinning of the drive wheels as the tractive effort collapsed. Double-headed 4–8–4 Greenbriers tugging at the head end and a Mallet shoving away behind the caboose could not get the long train started on its way.

Only when an 0–8–0 switcher was summoned to the rear of the train, hooked up to the Mallet's tender, and its strength added to the common endeavor, did

the train consent to begin moving up the grade. Once it did, the cab rocked and swayed as the Mallet worked powerfully away, the switch engine behind it huffing and chuffing as in tandem they rolled over the hill behind the train. Ten minutes later, having topped the crest of the rise and gained the downhill slope, the train eased to a stop.

In company with the superintendent of motive power I climbed down from the cab of the Mallet to the ground in the darkness. There were lines of hopper cars on either side of us as we set off down the track, while behind us the Mallet and the switch engine were uncoupled from the caboose and dropped back across the hill and back to the yard. We walked in the darkness until we came to an open area beyond the cars on the sidetrack and crossed over to a one-story office building, where there was an automobile waiting to drive us up to the head of the train and the waiting 4–8–4s a mile to the east.

We climbed up into the lead Greenbrier's cab, which was furnished with a considerably more formidable array of instruments, gauges, dials, knobs and handles than the relatively crude apparatus of the much older Mallet. We were ready to resume the run. The brakeman leaned out of the cab and signaled back along the train with a flashlight; the engineer reached up and pulled on a rope to sound the whistle twice; the air brakes went off; the throttle was notched; and the locomotives moved forward. There was no trouble with starting the train now; with the pistons blasting away we rolled ahead, bound for Hampton Roads and salt water.

———

Compared to the steam locomotive ride I had taken aboard the New York Central passenger train on the West Shore Division, this one involved notably less heat and dust. The firebox doors stayed closed, for the coal was fed from the tender to the fire by a mechanical stoker, so that the fireman had no shoveling duties to perform. Occasionally he checked the fire visually, but most of his work consisted of monitoring the array of gauges and dials and making occasional adjustments in terms of what the needles and pointers indicated. Up ahead, the headlamp illuminated the tracks, the adjacent right-of-way, and the pine trees. Whistling for crossings, we rocked along through the night. Occasionally we passed the headlights of automobiles waiting at crossroads for the long train to pass by. At various points along the double-track line there were sidings and stations—Providence Forge, Walker, Toano.

Twice down the track the headlamps of oncoming locomotives came into view, and I watched as they drew nearer. With a rush of air they swept past us, trains of empty coal cars in tow. The cars flashed by one after another, the air space between them creating a momentary expansion of sound as they raced past, until there came the lighted window of a caboose and the train slipped by. As it did I caught a brief glimpse of its rear platform; a trainman was waving a flashlight up and down to show that he was set to check the axles of the hopper cars of our train for hot boxes—overheated journal bearings—as they went past. Then we had the line all to ourselves again, and the headlamp beam reached out along the tracks into the night to light the way.

I remembered how as a child I had listened to the freight trains coming toward Charleston in the darkness, blowing for the crossings in St. Andrew's Parish, and had imagined how it would feel to be up in the locomotive cab and riding along with the train. This was what it would have been like.

The train maintained a steady pace eastward through the Virginia tidewater. Near the town—or more properly the crossroad—of Norge, there was a rise in the ruling grade, but the doubleheaded 4-8-4 locomotives breasted it in fine style, then rolled through the rock-cliff cut at the Williamsburg station and moved through pine forests and fields, until we were entering the outskirts of Newport News and the air brakes were released to clamp down upon the wheels and slow the long train's progress. The rails ahead branched out into a network of tracks, and we rolled into a train yard illuminated by floodlights, with lines of loaded hopper cars strung out alongside. Crawling along now, we passed by switch engines and more hopper cars, with the tracks bending southward, until at length we came to a halt not far from a two-story yard office building, and a signal tower not far away. It was close to midnight on a hot midsummer evening.

At the Hotel Warwick my room overlooked the water, and I could see the lights of Norfolk and Portsmouth far across, while off to the right were floodlights, cranes, and the superstructures and hulls of ships at the Newport News Shipbuilding and Drydock Company. I took a shower and got into bed, with the tempo of the train ride continuing to pulsate through my chest and in my head. It was a while before I went to sleep.

In the morning I was taken out onto the coaling piers, where I watched fifty-ton coal cars being moved along rails out alongside and above the sides of large ships. Clamped into the arms of a huge vise, they were lifted atop the open holds of large ship and turned upside down, to send the contents of the cars cascading down into the holds. Two ships were being loaded at a time. Anchored out in the Roadstead were others, empty and riding high, waiting their turn to take on coal.

I wrote three stories about the expedition, one on the trip aboard the coal train, one about the coal-loading, and another, for afternoon newspapers, about the overall operation. They were sent out on the wire and appeared in various newspapers, one of them in the Sunday *Richmond Times-Dispatch* and the *Baltimore Sun*. Meanwhile I went back to rewriting the carbons of the Richmond paper's news stories, and after that rewriting my own rewrites.

———

By then I had made up my mind to leave. I realized very well that I could not expect to walk into a newspaper job and not serve an apprenticeship. But I had not accepted a sizeable cut in pay and come to the Associated Press in order to spend my time doing nothing but rewriting other people's stories.

I knew that so far as being able to write went, I could hold my own with almost anybody I had ever worked with. The stories I wrote were published and read. This had been demonstrated up in New Jersey, and the C&O pieces I had done had shown that I had not lost the knack. I had been working as a newspaperman for two full years now, and was earning only a couple of dollars more a week than I had started out with in New Jersey. Whatever the newspaper etiquette and custom involved, I was not going to stay on a job at which I could not do what I was good at.

———

Without reasoning it out in so many words, what I wanted was a way to earn a living without having to divide my life into vocation and avocation. No doubt this was a great deal for a young man not yet turned 25 to ask, and no doubt I should have been more patient than I was. But as far as I was concerned, now that I was out of the Army there was no federal or state statute requiring me to remain at a job that I did not enjoy doing. I needed to find something that by aptitude and training I could perform competently, and that was also able to hold and sustain my interest.

I came to see in later years that an important part of the fascination locomotives and railroads held for me was that they symbolized that goal. Not that the trains were unworthy of full attention in their own right, of course. But their appeal for me also had much to do with the way in which their great energy was harnessed and put to good use. They, and in particular the steam locomotives, were purposeful, functional. They did the work they were designed to do, and with something left over for spectacle and show. They were not only efficient, but exciting to watch.

In the allurement they exerted on me I was by no means alone. I had the inspiration, and the example, of the novelist who at that time of my life meant most to

me. Thomas Wolfe, then only ten years dead, could write about riding on a railroad train this way:

> The boy felt the powerful movement of the train beneath him and the lonely austerity and mystery of the dark earth outside that swept past forever with a fanlike stroke, an immortal and imperturbable stillness. It seemed to him that these two terrific negatives of speed and stillness, the hurtling and projectile motion of the train and the calm silence of the everlasting earth, were poles of a single unity—a unity coherent with his destiny, whose source was somehow in himself.

It would be hard for me nowadays to explain exactly what all that meant, but like so much of what Thomas Wolfe wrote, it once spoke to me, and to numerous other young people of that era, with the thrilling discovery that thoughts and emotions that one had believed were private and unique to oneself were experienced and shared by others as well.

The same novel, *Of Time and the River,* opens with an episode 77 pages and 28,000 words long devoted entirely to a train trip between Asheville, North Carolina, and Baltimore, Maryland, in which there is a five-page account of the autobiographical protagonist, who has been drinking whiskey, as he stands in the vestibule between two railroad cars while the train speeds along. Wolfe sets out to describe the rocking of the coach and the sound of the wheels as they strike the rail joints, and the sudden commotion as another train passes on the adjacent track. "Rock, reel, smash, and swerve; hit it, hit it, on the curve; steady, steady does the trick, keep her steady as a stick," etc.

There is nothing to be gained from quoting the lengthy passage out of context. The point is that until I encountered this episode, it had never occurred to me that a writer of novels would ever have thought it worthwhile to record the emotions involved in that kind of experience. The fact that a writer *had* done so, and moreover had published it in a book—had made something worth reading out of it—was encouraging to a young would-be author who hadn't yet found out how to deploy his own emotional experience in his writing.

———

The idea came to me that I might leave newspaper work for a year for graduate study, where I could learn how to write publishable fiction. There were universities, I had read, where the writing of fiction and poetry was actually taught. As an Army veteran I was eligible for two more years of tuition and allowances to undertake graduate study. I wrote off to several universities. The writing program at the University of Iowa was the best-known of all, and moreover it was in the Midwest. I looked in the *Railway Guide*. The Rock Island, the Burlington, the Milwaukee Road, the Chicago &

Northwestern, the Union Pacific all passed within a few hours' drive of Iowa City. But the director of the Iowa program, Paul Engle, was willing to accept me on trial, for a term only. From the Johns Hopkins University in Baltimore I received an offer not only of admission into its graduate writing program, but a fellowship whereby I would be paid to teach a class in freshman composition and grammar.

So in early September of 1948 I loaded my belongings into my car and headed northward up U.S. Highway 301 for Baltimore, for what I thought would be a year of literary study before returning to newspaper work somewhere, and a job that would be more interesting and more fulfilling than anything I had found thus far.

Seven   A Discovery

After the first powerful plain manifesto,
The black statement of pistons, without more fuss
But gliding like a queen, she leaves the station
——Stephen Spender, "The Express"

I was going back into the North again. I was reminded of that when after driving across the Potomac River Bridge I stopped in a restaurant for lunch, and saw a row of slot machines along one wall. In the Commonwealth of Virginia during that era, if allowed on the premises they would have been in a back room, screened from immediate public view. But this was Maryland, where such things were openly countenanced. It was a small matter, yet it made me aware of the drastic nature of what I was now engaged in doing.

Unlike my initial excursion into New Jersey two years before, for this foray I had no fixed, established agenda, no simple, formulated goal—to be a reporter, to do so well at it that I would move on to a major daily newspaper in New York City, or the like. This time I knew that I wanted to write, and I wanted to have a try at writing fiction, but beyond that I was unsure of what to expect, and convinced only that what I had been doing thus far, in the two years since graduating from college, was not what I desired for a career. Whether what I was now about to try would take me closer to discovering a satisfactory vocation remained to be seen. But at least I had learned that much.

It occurred to me as odd that, just as two years earlier, it was when I moved out of the South, away from South Carolina and Virginia, that I became conscious of being part of something known as *Southern*. Living and working at home I did not often think of it one way or the other. But all it had taken was a casual stop for lunch in a restaurant located on the north side

of the Potomac River—in what, in fact, had during the Civil War probably been pro-Confederate territory—to make me aware of a tug upon my identity that until then had gone largely unnoticed. When I drove into downtown Baltimore I felt, to an extent, something like an invader entering unfamiliar territory.

The Pennsylvania Railroad and the Baltimore and Ohio were the two major railroads serving Baltimore. I had never ridden aboard the B&O, but during the war and on my previous stay in New Jersey I became familiar enough with the Pennsy's main line on trips to and from Richmond. What was there about the Pennsylvania Railroad that made me conscious of the fact that I was now in the North? I decided that it was the suburban commuter stations, with the iron railings between the northbound and southbound tracks, the red station signs with gold letters, and the seats along the platforms with the brightly lithographed Broadway theater posters. The first time I had seen them, riding in a troop shipment from Fort McClellan to New Haven in 1943, I had experienced the sensation of leaving the South for a new place.

From the standpoint of watching and photographing trains, the Raymond Loewy-designed GG-1's that pulled the clockers and the other through passenger trains on the Pennsy's electrified trackage were handsome enough, but not very interesting. The streamlined design left them devoid of individuality. There were also some PRR box-cab electrics that handled freight trains, and, being less bland and more

THE ROUTE OF
The
BLACK
DIAMOND

rugose in appearance, these were more photogenic. The Pennsylvania branch to Harrisburg, however, where it connected with the main line westward from Philadelphia, was not electrified, and both diesel-electrics and steam locomotives were used on it, including some husky-looking 4–4–2 Atlantics that pulled local passenger trains and, by comparison with the graceful, high-wheeled 4–4–2's that I had seen handling commuter trains in northern New Jersey, were as bulldogs to whippets.

It was the Baltimore and Ohio, however, that quickly drew my attention. The majority of its locomotives were still steam, not diesel-powered. The freight locomotives operating out of Baltimore were sturdy, handsome 2–8–2 Mikados, with rounded Vanderbilt tenders like those on the Seaboard's, but lacking the array of booster tanks and boxes mounted on the front of the smoke boxes of the Seaboard 2–8–2s. Passenger trains and way freights were pulled both by diesels and several varieties of 4–6–2 Pacifics.

There were two B&O passenger stations, connected by a tunnel beneath downtown Baltimore. The Mount Royal Station, located several blocks from Penn Station, was one of the most interesting I had ever seen. Situated next to a hillside, it was built of stone, with a lofty tower, and it had a waiting room with rocking chairs and wicker furniture next to an arched train shed, and the waiting area was separated from the tracks by a high wrought-iron gate. Trains entered from tunnels at either end. To watch from close up as a 4–6–2 arrived from New York and Philadelphia, en route to Washington, with a train of day coaches and dining, club, and parlor cars, was a memorable sight. It seemed almost to erupt in a crescendo of smoke and steam when it emerged from the tunnel. It blasted into the station and across the train shed, until the locomotive drew to a halt at the entrance to the far tunnel that led underneath the downtown city.

The B&O's New York-to-Washington trains, in particular the Royal Blue, were far more comfortable to travel in than the coaches on the Pennsylvania Railroad.

Instead of the hard plush upright seats of the clockers and the customary rush to find vacant places, there were individually reserved, reclining seats with headrests and ample footroom. The Royal Blue's dining car, with linen tablecloths, gleaming tableware and vases with flowers, and white china with a blue railroad motif, served excellent meals, in particular a magnificent tossed salad. Once I boarded the Royal Blue at Mount Royal and rode on it to Washington just to have dinner in the dining car. The B&O's trackage to Washington was notably smoother than the Pennsy's much-pounded roadbed (so rough was the latter that the dining-car waiters were always careful to pour only a half-cup of coffee at a time).

The PRR enjoyed only one advantage over the B&O—but that one was crucial. Its trains went directly into New York City via the tunnel under the Hudson River, making the Washington-to-New York trip in four hours and five minutes. The B&O trains, operating over Jersey Central trackage north of Philadelphia, terminated at Jersey City, where passengers boarded buses that crossed the river via ferry and were borne to locations in Manhattan. The trip required more than five hours. The ride was comfortable, pleasant, in every way superior to that on the crowded, grubby PRR trains. But most travelers between Washington and New York were uninterested in scenery, and they were willing to put up with crowded coaches and hard, upright double-seats in order to get where they were going in an hour's less time.

In the years after the first World War the B&O trains used Penn Station and the tunnel under the Hudson River, too, but in 1926 they changed to Jersey City and the ferry across the river. It was a losing battle: the greater comfort of the B&O trains could not overcome the handicap. Finally, in 1958, the B&O canceled the Royal Blue, gave up its New York-to-Washington service, and thereafter operated its trains only from Baltimore to Washington and the Midwest. That, however, lay in the future, and while I was living in Baltimore and working and teaching at Johns

Hopkins I made a point of riding the B&O whenever I could.

The B&O's yards and shops were located south of downtown Baltimore, near the Camden Station. It was there that the first steam locomotive in America performed in 1831. In 1832 the line was extended to Point of Rocks, on the Potomac River, and thereafter westward. One afternoon I drove to Point of Rocks, about sixty miles by auto from Baltimore, and stationed myself just beyond the attractive, steepled station with gabled roof, where the Baltimore and Washington tracks diverged. I photographed a Baltimore-bound freight train with a 2–8–2 Mikado at the head and another behind the caboose. An eastbound passenger local, pulled by a light 4–6–2 Pacific, came along, stopped briefly at the station, then headed for Washington. Then the all-coach Columbian arrived from Washington en route to Chicago, diesel engines at the head and with six stainless steel coaches, including one with a low dome, the first east of the Mississippi. It clipped through the junction and on toward Chicago, 750 miles away, where it was scheduled in a little after eight the following morning.

There was another railroad, the Western Maryland, hauling coal from the mountains to Baltimore. It also operated several commuter passenger trains between Baltimore and Emmitsburg, Maryland. I got one good photograph of a 4–6–2 Pacific, equipped with platform steps for freight brakemen's use, engaged in hauling a line of day coaches out of Penn Station.

By far the most unusual train putting in at Baltimore, however, was the daily passenger service on the Ma and Pa—the Maryland and Pennsylvania, which ran between Baltimore and York, Pennsylvania, along a winding 77-mile-long route, as contrasted with the Pennsylvania's 57. I found the station just off North Avenue, several blocks from Penn Station, down a flight of stairs from the viaduct over the Patapsco River floodplain. A pert little 4–4–0 built in 1901, with high domes and a huge headlamp atop the smoke box, was waiting to haul a train consisting of a baggage car and a single day coach. Nearby were several boxcars and a caboose, the latter remarkable for having only two sets of wheels.

I found that it was possible to board the Ma and Pa early afternoon train, ride it to York, then catch a Pennsylvania train back to Baltimore. So the following Saturday I made the run. The route of the Ma and Pa snaked northward along the Green Spring Valley of Maryland. "Snaked" is precisely the term, for the road bed had originally been surveyed and constructed for a narrow-gauge line, then before the operation actually began the trackage was changed to standard 4 feet, 8 ½ inch width. The sharper curves meant that equipment had to be restricted in length and train speed kept low.

The little locomotive puffed its way industriously along, its whistle sounding shrilly as it approached grade crossings. There were stations with names like Notch Cliff, Glen Arm, Laurel Brook, Fern Cliff, Vale, Sharon, The Rocks, Minefield, and Pylesville. When the train made a stop, one or two persons might get on or off, and sometimes the baggage man handled a package or two. Eventually we crossed over the state line and entered the Pennsylvania Dutch country. One of the more important stops was at Red Lion, a cigar-making center and the originator of a pungent stogie whose only rival for cheap bliss was the notorious Uncle Willie of Baltimore manufacture. It was also famous as the home of the girl whose life was saved from blight by a kindly Baltimore madam, as chronicled in H. L. Mencken's delightful sketch, "The Girl from Red Lion, Pa." After several other stops we arrived at York, where the four-hour-long journey ended. By then it was dark. After dinner I boarded a Pennsylvania train, and in less than an hour and a half was back at Penn Station in Baltimore.

———

I should say at once that I did not learn how to write novels at Johns Hopkins that year. It would be another twelve years before I published a novel, and although I later published two others and some stories, the writing of fiction did not turn out to be my long suit. The very naivete of my plan, the notion that someone could take a year off and learn how to write fiction, in the way that one could be taught how to play an accordion or to drive a truck, shows how much I still had to learn about my own capabilities or, for that matter, where my true interests lay. What I did find out, however, was that it was at and in universities, not newsrooms, that the kind of writing and thinking that came most naturally to my particular set of aptitudes was best done. It would be several years before the full implications of that discovery sunk through my skull, but I had begun to see the point.

That winter I did put my interest in trains and in writing fiction to brief commercial use. Living on a very tight budget, I decided one evening to try writing a short story for *Railroad Magazine*, which at the time was aimed principally at railroad people. I worked up a melodramatic tale about a boomer—an engineer who moves from job to job—who disgraces himself by reporting for work drunk, but redeems his reputation and self-respect by piloting a logging train on a perilous run through a snowstorm in the Far Northwest. I had never been within three thousand miles of the Far Northwest, nor ever laid eyes on a logging railroad, but the story was accepted and a check for $40 arrived in the mail. I promptly knocked out two more stories about the same character. Both were returned. So ended my career as an author of pulp fiction. That kind of writing was simple stuff, done by formula. The fiction I was learning to admire at Johns Hopkins involved the exploration of character, and to understand and write it required psychological insight. There was no formula available, and I was a long way from mastering its workings.

I did not want to leave Baltimore and the university. I wanted to keep studying and learning, and I had made friends among both the faculty and the graduate students. But the writing program was for the master's degree only, and I had no wish to continue for a doctorate in the English Department, which was a pedantic operation uninterested in the writing of the twentieth century. So as the close of the school year approached, I went looking for a newspaper position within easy range of Baltimore. I located one on the copy desk of the morning paper in Wilmington, Delaware, an hour away by train. The thought was that I would find a routine job that I could perform more or less mechanically, and save my imaginative involvement for the kind of writing I now intended to do—fiction, poetry, literary criticism. Presumably I now knew where I was headed.

I should have known better. I was no more prepared to separate what I did for a living from my imaginative interests than I had been before I began graduate school. Nor was I able to work in a vacuum, without friends who shared my professional interests. Instead of using my afternoons to write—my newspaper hours were from five P.M. to midnight, five days a week— I read books or else went looking for trains. My colleagues on the copy desk and the staff were all older than myself, and uninterested in writing and writers. The one exception was the city editor, who came from a Virginia family and was much interested in Civil War history; we became lifelong friends. But he was fifteen years older than I and married.

Sometimes when I finished up work I would drive over to the Pennsylvania Railroad station and watch the trains arrive and depart until two or three A.M. In addition to the New York–Washington line, the Delmarva division of the Pennsy operated through Delaware and the Eastern Shore of Maryland and Virginia to the mouth of the Chesapeake Bay, then by ferry to Norfolk. There was a passenger train that arrived from Philadelphia and departed for Cape Charles some time after one A.M. I watched while the GG-1 electric was uncoupled and a steam locomotive, usually a 4–4–2 Atlantic, backed into the station and hooked up to the coaches. There was a long wait before the train, which had very few patrons, chugged out of the station, the glare from its firebox prominently visible in the darkness at the end of the platform. I wanted to go along.

Some mornings and afternoons I drove over into Pennsylvania, and photographed trains on the Lehigh Valley, the Reading, and the Jersey Central. The B&O had freight yards at Wilmington and I photographed some trains there. But what I wanted was to be back at Johns Hopkins.

Fortunately, those in charge wanted me back. The chairman of the Writing Seminars offered to find a couple of courses for me to teach in the evening adult education program. I had another eight months of eligibility for veterans' educational benefits. I could pick up a little money writing feature stories. I would be cutting it close—but doing what I wanted to be doing, where I wished to be. The future would have to take care of itself.

———

The Sunday section of the *Richmond Times-Dispatch* paid fifteen to twenty-five dollars for a story. A couple of such checks could substantially augment my monthly income. I went home to my parents on weekends from time to time, and I wrote about anything I could think of that might interest the Sunday editor.

The Richmond, Fredericksburg and Potomac Railroad was a corporation, the shares in which were owned by the State of Virginia. It handled all rail traffic between the Northeast and the South Atlantic seaboard, and I arranged to do a two-part feature on it. One of the oldest railroads in the nation, it remained totally powered by steam. Its roster of recently built 2–8–4's and 4–8–4's, named after Virginia generals and governors, operated between the Washington Union Station and the Potomac Yards at Alexandria, and Broad Street Station and the Acca and Hermitage Yards in Richmond. In addition to the north-south trains of the Atlantic Coast Line and the Seaboard Air Line, the RF&P had its own passenger and freight runs.

In one story I described its history, interviewed its chief management, and wrote about how it was faring economically and what its future plans and prospects

were. The other story—the one that I wanted to write—was devoted to a ride in the cab of a locomotive from Richmond to Washington. I had been aboard locomotive cabs in the past, but never on a really fast passenger run. I boarded the Governor Patrick Henry, a 4–8–4 Northern locomotive, at Broad Street Station. The supervisor who accompanied me offered me the use of a pair of gloves, a pair of goggles, and a cap. I declined all but the goggles. At 12:20 P.M. the engineer moved the reverse gear in, engaged the throttle, and we eased forward with a twelve-car train in tow. By the time we had cleared the Richmond yards and were swinging past the golf course at Laurel the speed indicator was showing 58 miles an hour. A long double-headed freight train passed by, headed south.

We slowed up for a station stop at Ashland, where the tracks ran right down the main street and past the campus of Randolph-Macon College. I remembered being taken by my father on the train from Richmond to Ashland, then returning on an interurban, which as far as I was concerned was no more than a large trolley car and not nearly so impressive as the railroad coach. The interurban was now long gone, although the trestle over which it operated to its terminal in downtown Richmond was still in existence.

We resumed our run, picking up speed as we went. Within a few miles north of Ashland we were making 70 miles an hour, when a signal block alongside the tracks showed yellow. The road operated under centralized track control, and the engineer had six seconds in which to acknowledge the signal or the locomotive would automatically come to a stop. We slowed to 25 miles an hour. I was told that the cause was very likely the C&O's westbound Sportsman engaged in crossing the line at Doswell. I thought of the occasion, three years earlier, when, returning home from New Jersey, I was aboard a southbound train that spent long hours stalled north of Doswell. This time there was only a brief slow order before the signal again showed the track clear, and by the time we reached and passed Doswell we were back at full speed.

The sensation of all-out running, with the drive wheels pounding and the whistle shrieking for crossings, was exhilarating, even though the roadbed was so smooth that there was little or no rocking motion in the cab—which, since the Governor Patrick Henry and its tender weighed something like 660,000 pounds, was just as well. The grade over Rutherglen Hill reduced our speed to 62 miles an hour, but once over it we were soon doing 70 again. Near Fredericksburg we passed the white cottage where Stonewall Jackson had died after being wounded by his own men during the battle of Chancellorsville.

At Aquia Creek, where before the Civil War the RF&P had terminated and passengers had boarded steamboats to continue to Washington via the Potomac River, there was a new bridge in place that enabled the train to maintain its speed; until the previous year it had been necessary to slow down to 35. Before long, however, we encountered another slow order, and were forced to creep through a construction area at 10 miles an hour.

After stopping at Alexandria across from the national Masonic George Washington Memorial Tower, we passed by the Potomac Yards, which interchanged freight cars between the ACL, Seaboard, Southern, C&O, B&O and Pennsylvania railroads. We crossed the Potomac River, moved through a cut behind various federal government buildings, then entered a long tunnel. I had been through it numerous times while inside coaches, but never in an open locomotive cab. After a few minutes the locomotive and train emerged from the tunnel into Union Station, and we came to a stop alongside a train platform. We were exactly thirty seconds behind schedule.

I returned the borrowed goggles. "Now run your fingers through your hair," the superintendent said. I did so. My scalp was well sprinkled with specks of soot and ash. "Told you you should have used that cap," he said.

The Governor Patrick Henry was uncoupled and rumbled off toward the locomotive facilities at Ivy City, where it would be groomed for a southbound run that evening. It was a magnificent piece of machinery, somewhat lightweight as Northerns went but perfectly fitted to the trains and the right-of-way. There were twenty-six similar steam locomotives on the RF&P's roster, as well as many other kinds. They constituted as up-to-date and efficient a train-hauling force as any in the United States. That within less than a decade all would be replaced by diesels would have been difficult to credit.

If the RF&P's fleet of 4–8–4's and 2–8–4's represented the latest in modern steam locomotion, I also had a look that winter at small-time railroading—very small-time. The Nelson and Albemarle Railroad, a short line operating between Schuyler, Esmont, and Warren, Virginia, where it connected with the C&O's James River Division, announced that it was discontinuing passenger service, and I went along with the Old Dominion Railway Club for the last ride. The line was thirteen miles long, and the motive power consisted of a small 2–6–2 locomotive. Since it never ventured far from its home base, the locomotive had no need of a tender. The water it used for its boiler was carried in a saddle tank draped over the boiler and smoke box, and a bin about three feet wide welded onto the back of the cab bore quite enough coal for a day's operations.

The passenger coach, a combine which also housed the baggage compartment, had green plush seats, oil lamps, and a potbellied stove. The passenger fare to make the entire trip and the return to Schuyler came to forty-five cents. The right-of-way led past old quarries, high cuts, hills and rolling fields, with the tracks groaning and swaying on the crossties as the train steamed by. Upon reaching Esmont, the locomotive, which had headlamps and cowcatchers front and back, moved onto a sidetrack and around the coach, then coupled itself onto the other end, and, running backwards, returned to Schuyler for another load. Returning, we set out to Warren. On the way a pair of deer, frightened by the commotion, raced along beside the locomotive for a half-mile, vaulting gracefully over wire fences before finally veering off into

A Memory of Trains

the woods. Various people got on and off the train, in order to be present for the last run. The total fare collected by the conductor for the occasion came to $17.71, which he said was the biggest day's passenger business the N&A had done in many a day.

I also tracked down and wrote a story on the Church Hill Tunnel cave-in of 1925, in which a C&O work train had been working in a old tunnel under Church Hill, east of the Shockoe Valley in Richmond. After having been idle since the turn of the century, the tunnel was being refurbished to permit freight cars to bypass the Main Street Station and move directly to Fulton Yard. There had been warnings that the terrain above the old tunnel might be unstable, but the C&O authorities assumed that the roof of the shaft could be properly shored up with timbers. The work train had moved into the tunnel at an early hour one morning and several hundred workmen were beginning their labors, when earth began to fall from the tunnel roof near the western entrance. The electric lights in the tunnel flickered off, and more earth began dropping. Most of the work force sprinted for the eastern end of the tunnel. The conductor, a brakeman, and most of the laborers managed to get out, but the engineer and at least two laborers were trapped inside the tunnel.

Ultimately the engineer's body was recovered, but additional earth slides halted further work. Nobody knew exactly how many bodies might remain inside. Two were definitely unaccounted for, but some who had made it out safely insisted that other black laborers had come into the western entrance to the tunnel not long before the cave-in, looking for work. The tunnel was filled in with sand and its entrances sealed off, leaving a 4-4-0 work locomotive and ten flat cars permanently in place under Church Hill, along with at least two unrecovered bodies.

I located and interviewed the conductor of the work train, a man in his sixties, and quoted from contemporary accounts of the disaster in the newspaper files. A ballad had been written about the cave-in, and I quoted from the lyrics. After each verse came a chorus:

Brothers keep shovelin',
Pickin' in the ground.
Brothers, keep listening
For the train that's never been found.

As with most railroad ballads, the details were not exactly accurate. The train itself had been found, its location was known exactly, and the body of the engineer had been removed from the cab. If anything was permanently lost it was the sheet music to the song, which I had seen when I copied the lyrics for my story but has since vanished entirely. In the mid-1980s a former student of mine, Katie Letcher Lyle, at work on a book about railroad wreck songs, undertook an extensive search for the missing music, but without success.

———

For a writer who was greatly interested in railroads and railroading, to have an article published in *Trains Magazine* constituted a kind of certification of competence. True, it did not pay very much, but it was the publication that all railroad enthusiasts read. So I was much pleased when I was able to arrange with the editor of *Trains* to write a piece on the Atlantic and Danville Railway, a single-track road that operated along the Virginia–North Carolina border and Southside Virginia.

For fifty years, from 1899 to 1949, the A&D had been leased by the Southern Railway and operated as part of the Southern system. In the early 1950s, however, with passenger revenues dwindling and freight service suffering from the inroads of highway truck transportation, the Southern was attempting to divest itself of some of its less lucrative properties, and the Interstate Commerce Commission was showing itself more willing than in earlier years to countenance such divestments. The Southern decided not to renew the Danville-to-Tidewater lease, and the A&D's trustees set out to operate it independently.

ICC approval was secured to drop the single, seldom-used daily passenger train, which was costing the Southern $100,000 a year to keep running. The road got rid of the old 2–8–0 Consolidation steam locomotives inherited from the Southern, purchased six new Alco-GE 1500–hp. road-switcher diesels, and instituted overnight freight service from Danville to Portsmouth, on the Elizabeth River and Hampton Roads. Within a year the three- and four-car trains that had customarily constituted the A&D's payload had become strings of up to forty cars or more, making it necessary to doublehead the Alco locomotives.

To make the run, on a Sunday afternoon I rode the Southern Railway's daily passenger train from Hull Street Station in South Richmond down to Danville. A single diesel road-switcher was at the head end. This was the original trackage of the Richmond and Danville–Richmond Terminal Company line from which, in 1894, the financier J. P. Morgan had developed the Southern system through consolidations, purchases, and leases. Less than thirty years before that, Jefferson Davis and his cabinet had fled from Richmond to Danville along the route, when the Confederate States of America was disintegrating around them. It was at Danville where Old 97 had come to grief on September 27, 1903, when it jumped the tracks on a trestle leading over the Dan River and plunged into a creek bed, leaving engineer Steve Brodie "with his hand on the throttle / scalded to death by the steam." Five others also died.

When I got off the train in Danville a 2–8–2 Mikado was hauling a northbound Southern freight through the station, and a three-unit cream-and-green EMD diesel was waiting nearby at the head of southbound Southern passenger train No. 35, the Washington-Atlanta-New Orleans Express. On a side track at the depot, I found the A&D caboose. The conductor and flagman were expecting me.

It was turning dark by the time that two black-and-white A&D Alco diesel locomotives backed along the track to the caboose, coupled up, and pulled us over to the yards. An eleven-car train was waiting to make the overnight trip. The flagman assured me that the consist was the fewest the train had hauled in some time; they had brought in forty-one cars that morning.

For the first twenty miles of the 207–mile run, A&D train No. 86 wove back and forth across the Virginia–North Carolina state line. I stationed myself in the cupola and watched the lead locomotive's beam illuminating the tracks eleven cars ahead. The conductor finished checking his waybills, then measured a generous supply of coffee into a large enameled pot and set it upon the lid of a potbellied stove. He tossed chunks of wood into the stove, splashed a little kerosene on them, and applied a match.

There were no other trains working anywhere along the A&D main line that night. On weekday nights a train operated in each direction, but a single train made the run from Hampton Roads to Danville on Saturday night and returned on Sunday. We were in the bright-leaf tobacco country, and we moved through seemingly endless rows of tobacco in adjacent fields. At Denniston, Virginia, we set a gondola car loaded with scrap iron on a siding for the Norfolk and Western to collect, then picked up five cars of cement.

When the coffee was ready the brakeman declined to drink any of it. "Not for me," he said. "The captain makes good railroad coffee—when you can drop a track spike into it and it floats, the coffee's done." It was an ancient railroad joke, but I drank a cup with pleasure, for the evening was becoming chilly. West of Clarksville, Virginia, the train moved onto Southern trackage for several miles. We were in the area along the Virginia–North Carolina line that was scheduled to be part of the Buggs Island reservoir—in North Carolina it was known as Kerr Lake—and the A&D's right-of-way was in the process of being relocated beyond the watershed several miles to the north. Within a couple of years' time the roadbed along which we were now moving would be under water.

At Jeffress, Virginia, we moved onto a siding and picked up five cars, three of them loaded with pulpwood. While the switching was being done I left the caboose and walked up to the cab of the lead loco-motive to ride in it for a while. We gained a car and lost one at South Hill, Virginia, and proceeded to LaCrosse, Virginia, where the main line of the Seaboard intersected. There we dropped off an empty hopper car, and I returned to the caboose.

Thirty-five minutes later and we were at Lawrenceville, where the A&D maintained its shops and operating headquarters. I looked around to see whether any of the old 2–8–0 steam locomotives might still be on hand, but although a water tank was still in place alongside the tracks, all I saw were two more Alco diesels. Another twenty miles and we were at Emporia, where the A&D trackage crossed the Atlantic Coast Line main line. We set out two cars and picked up five cars loaded with highway cement.

By then it was three A.M., and not even the conductor's potent railroad coffee was proving suffi-cient to keep my eyes open. So when I was invited to stretch out on a canvas-covered cot I did not argue, and within minutes I was asleep. I scarcely noticed when we reached Franklin, Virginia, where there were paper mills, and dropped off the pumpwood cars. Not until we came to Suffolk, at about five A.M., did I wake up. The locomotives were setting out a boxcar and a tank car. It was soon turning light, and we moved through the flat country of the Virginia tidewater, with occa-sional stretches of salt marsh.

Now we were entering onto Atlantic Coast Line trackage, and A&D train No. 86 halted on a curve outside of Portsmouth to pick up a set of train orders. The brakeman set out a red flare to warn of our pres-ence, then we proceeded to the yards at Pinner's Point, on the Elizabeth River opposite Norfolk. It was a few minutes after six A.M. and we were right on schedule. The conductor stopped the train at a strategic spot to allow me to take a bus downtown. Later that morning I talked with the A&D's management.

Though hardly an exciting ride—at no time did the train move at speeds higher than 35 or 40 miles an hour—I had found it quite intriguing. I had been able

to observe at first hand just how railroad freight service operated. On a bigger railroad with a longer string of cars and a faster schedule, there would have been no operations on sidings, and no setting out and picking up cars for delivery along the line. Switching locomo-tives would have been present for that. But these train-men had done everything for themselves—thrown the switches, spotted the cars on sidings, added new cars to the consist, operated their freight train across the A&D's entire main line, all 207 miles of it—even if I had been sound asleep for a two-hour stretch of the run.

Publication of the article that fall happened hand-ily. I had gone over to Washington from Baltimore with a girlfriend to see a play, and when we returned to Washington Union Station we passed by a newsstand. On display was the copy of *Trains* with my article, which I had not yet seen. I bought two copies and presented her with one of them.

Today the Atlantic and Danville is long gone. Once the major railroad mergers began in the 1960s, there was no more point in operating an independent single-track road between Danville and Norfolk. There were too many other ways to move freight to and from Hampton Roads. So the A&D disappeared into his-tory. Even the trackage was taken up and the right-of-way abandoned.

———

The previous summer, while I was working in Delaware, I had read a new book, a collection of sto-ries by Eudora Welty entitled *The Golden Apples.* That winter I read it again, and the more I thought about it, the more fascinating it seemed. The stories took place in a Mississippi town over the course of forty years. The writer whose fiction had meant most to me, Thomas Wolfe, was likewise a Southerner, from North Carolina, and I had been able to recognize certain scenes and characters in his novels that markedly resembled my own experience of growing up in South Carolina. What had attracted me most in Thomas Wolfe, however, was the depiction, which was obviously autobiographical, of the young protagonist as he grew up and left the small Southern city to seek fulfillment in the metropolis and in Europe. There was much about the excitement of riding on trains, which I found especially intriguing; so much of it was like my own experience of trains.

Now, with Eudora Welty's fiction, I found something else; I was caught up in the involvements and entanglements of the people in the imagined Mississippi town. Their doings and their thoughts were made every bit as complex and as full of imagination and mystery as the best fiction I had ever read by Leo Tolstoy or James Joyce or any of the great European masters. I began to notice and to think about why it was that Wolfe and Welty, although they were very different kinds of writers, seemed to share certain ways of thinking about people, and writing about them, that had to do with their both being Southern.

In another novel by Eudora Welty, *Delta Wedding*, a train also figured, but it was not at all like those in Wolfe. It did not bear a young man away from the small Southern town toward the distant metropolis. Instead it puffed along the Mississippi Delta countryside. It was comic—but it was also dangerous. It reminded me of the little gas-electric train I used to see puttering along near Hampton Park in Charleston, the Boll Weevil.

———

That spring I was offered a full-time instructorship at the university. I was to teach three courses, one of them the graduate fiction workshop. I had yet to publish any literary fiction of my own, and I was dubious. "Don't worry," the chairman assured me, "you can handle it." My salary was not much higher than I had made as a beginning newspaperman, but it was for twelve months a year while teaching only nine; and if I taught in the summer school I could earn a little more. There was no commitment beyond the forthcoming school year of 1950–1951. No matter.

Without intending to be, without ever having thought of making it into my career, I was now a teacher. I was being paid to read and talk—and write—about books and writing. I had happened onto it by accident, stumbled into it almost. Yet during the forty years that followed, I would never grow tired of doing it.

Eight The Route of the Boll Weevil

> Every few minutes the little train brought us to a standstill in one of the stations which came before Balbec-Plage, stations the mere names of which (Incarville, Marcouville, Doville, Pont-à-Coulevre, Arambouville, Saint-Mars-le-Vieux, Hermonville, Maineville) seemed to me outlandish, whereas if I had come upon them in a book I should have at once been struck by their affinity to the names of certain places in the neighborhood of Combray.
>
> —Marcel Proust, *Remembrance of Things Past*

I was planning a visit to Charleston that summer, and the idea came to me that instead of going down on the Havana Special as I usually did, this might be a chance, after all these years, to ride on the Boll Weevil. I checked a Seaboard timetable, and trains No. 25 and 26 were still listed as running daily between Hamlet and Savannah via Charleston, one each way. I could take a Seaboard Air Line train from Richmond to Hamlet, stay there overnight, and the next morning ride down to Charleston on the little gas-electric train. For all its familiar presence during my growing-up years, I had never once photographed it, much less ridden aboard it.

I would make an expedition of it. The Silver Meteor left Richmond at 7:30 P.M. and arrived in Hamlet at 12:15 A.M., with stops at Petersburg and Raleigh. I had never ridden in the lead cab of a diesel-electric locomotive at the head of a fast passenger train, so I arranged with the Sunday editor of the *Richmond Times-Dispatch* to write a feature story about a ride on the Meteor. I made a reservation at the railroad hotel across from the Hamlet station. I would spend the night there, and in the morning go aboard the Boll Weevil.

It would be an interesting contrast: the crack New York-to-Florida all-reserved-seat main-line express with its lengthy string of stainless steel coaches, and the small gas-electric combine, which ever since I could remember had gone clicking its way along the Charleston branch, seemingly in no hurry to reach its destination and with little about it that would cause anyone to mark its passage. The Meteor's schedule called for it to cover the 257 miles between Richmond and Hamlet in four hours and a half, averaging 56 miles an hour; the Boll Weevil would take six hours to travel from Hamlet to Charleston, a run of 167 miles, or an average of not quite 28 miles an hour if on time—which according to my recollections it frequently was not.

At last I would be seeing all the little towns and hamlets whose names I used to read and wonder about. When a teenager I had picked up copies of the orange-covered Seaboard Air Line timetable at the station, and I would read in it and think about the places where the Boll Weevil would be stopping after it left Charleston for Hamlet: Yeaman's Hall and Inness and Cordesville and Witherby and Bethera and Oceda and Warsaw and Hemingway and Johnsonville and

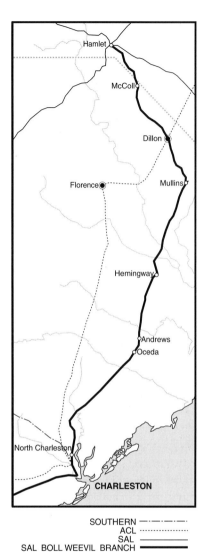

SOUTHERN —·—·—·—
ACL ··················
SAL ────
SAL BOLL WEEVIL BRANCH ━━━━━

So I rode down to my parents' home in Richmond—they were pleased with my having a full-time job again, though less than enchanted with the salary I would be receiving—and on the appointed evening I watched the Meteor pull into the elevated tracks of Main Street Station. I handed my ticket to the conductor and made my way up to the head of the train. A road foreman of locomotives was there to meet me. We climbed up into the cab of the lead locomotive, and within minutes the signal came to depart.

We headed out along the trestle, crossed over the old Chesapeake and Ohio canal and the tracks of the C&O's James River Division, and over the James River. The boulders and slabs of the fall line that made the river impassable upstream to ships were in twilight view far below. The Southern Railway tracks to the West Point branch and two automobile spans crossed the river not far away. From the cab of the EMD road diesel, located at the very front of the locomotive and open on three sides, the view of the tracks ahead was superior to that from the steam locomotives I had ridden. The headlamp wove a steady figure-eight upon the right-of-way and the adjacent scenery. The noise of the engines behind us, sealed off by a compartment, was moderate, considerably less loud in fact than what was heard outside when diesels passed by.

Although there was the definite feel of fast travel after the train cleared South Richmond and the DuPont plant and began running wide open, unlike what had been true aboard the RF&P's steam-powered 4–8–4 I had little sense of all-out running. And there were no tiny particles of soot or ash in the air. It was warm in the cab, but for all the grit and ash I noticed, we might have been driving along in a truck. The road foreman of engines, indeed, was wearing a business suit.

There was really very little for the fireman to do other than occasionally to check the assortment of indicator gauges. As for the engineer, he sat looking straight up the tracks ahead, his vision unimpeded by any locomotive barrel and smoke box. One foot, I was

Eulonia and Centenary and Koonce and Halavon and Clio and Green Pond—above all, Hamlet itself. What an odd name for a town to have. Why, they might even have named it Elsinore. Was there a cliff there that beetled o'er its base toward the sea? Hardly— though far back in geological time the Sandhills region of the coastal plain where Hamlet lay had been the shore of the ocean. Now I would see what there was to see.

told, was at all times kept pressed upon what was called the "dead man's throttle," a pedal which must always be held down. If ever the pressure were removed and the pedal allowed to rise up, the train would be brought to an immediate halt.

It was interesting to watch the various stations, grade crossings, and towns go by as we swept along in the darkness, seeing the block signals loom and disappear, and spotting the occasional headlamp of a train up ahead on a siding. The southbound Silver Meteor took priority over all other Seaboard trains except the northbound section. We made a stop at Petersburg, then crossed the Appomattox River along a high trestle. Below was the Norfolk and Western main line, but it was too dark now to catch sight of it. We were heading for Southside Virginia. Beyond LaCrosse, after the tracks crossed the Atlantic and Danville right-of-way, we passed the waiting northbound Palmland, its lighted coach windows no more than a bright blur as we cruised by at 62 miles an hour. Twice we encountered the red lanterns of cabooses and sped past freight trains that had moved off the main line to let us go by.

———

The Meteor pulled into Hamlet at 1:15 A.M. I walked down the platform toward the railroad hotel. In the lobby were the usual potted palms and somewhat frayed lounge chairs, the latter devoid at that hour of occupants. There were no outside telephones in the rooms, the clerk said, but I could be given a wakeup buzzer over an internal phone system. The Boll Weevil was scheduled to leave for Charleston at 9:45 A.M. I left a call for 8:30.

My room was on the second floor, without bath or running water. A large washbowl and pitcher were in place atop a bureau. An open window fronted on the brick wall of a building.

All night long there was the sound of trains. Hamlet was where the Seaboard line to Atlanta and Birmingham, on which I had ridden during my days

at Fort Benning, split off from the line to Florida. In addition to its being the terminus for the Hamlet-Charleston-Savannah branch, another branch, between Wilmington and Charlotte, also crossed the main line at Hamlet. Trains, diesel- and steam-powered both, clanged into town and through it. All of them passed by the passenger station. Whistles sounded from far off, drew near; steam hissed, revolving locomotive bells tumbled, couplers clanked, chains rattled, box cars clinked and jolted. Whenever a train came through the intersection outside the hotel the crossing alarm bell began sounding. I wondered which of the numerous freight trains I heard had crossed the wooden trestle over the Ashley River and moved through Charleston earlier that evening.

Eventually I fell asleep and stayed asleep. The in-house buzzer on the wall vibrated to awaken me in the morning. I ate breakfast at the hotel coffee shop, then, suitcase in hand, set out for the station. I walked along the long concrete platform, past cross-tracks with a diesel locomotive and a 4–8–2 Mountain type at the heads of trains. The Boll Weevil was not yet in place.

The station was an unusual-looking two-story wooden structure with a wide pointed dome that resembled a rain hat, and with overhanging roofs on both stories. At the window inside the waiting room I bought a ticket to Charleston, and asked when train No. 25 would be ready. "It's loading now," the agent said.

I went outside. "Where's the Charleston train?" I asked a nearby trainman.

He pointed toward the diesel locomotive I had just seen.

I had waited too long.

———

The red-and-yellow diesel-electric that had taken the place of the little gas-electric combine was a Baldwin model, smaller than the Electro-Motive road units that pulled the Silver Meteor and other main-line Seaboard trains. It was a single unit only, with a prominent horn protruding forward from the top of the cab like the barrel of a 37mm antitank gun. Behind it were a baggage car and a single day coach. The old 4–8–2 that was wheezing sand hissing across from it headed a somewhat longer train that would shortly be departing for Wilmington, 111 miles to the east.

I took a few photographs and went into the single day coach, which was air-conditioned, with reclining blue seats, and divided into separate compartments for whites and blacks. There were only a couple of other passengers. I set my suitcase on an overhead rack, then stepped out onto the rear vestibule. Not far away was an unpaved street of white sand. So bright was the sunshine upon it that it was difficult to tell which was the more dazzling, the reflection off the packed silica of the sand or that off the gleaming steel rails. Overhead the sky was clear blue.

A pickup truck was coming along the street toward the station, its tires kicking up white dust. Three men were standing next to the vestibule of a coach on the Wilmington train, conversing in low tones. Their bodies cast long shadows on the ground; it was still more than three hours before noontime. The truck rattled past. It was just as well that the coach was air-conditioned, as the Boll Weevil would probably not have been. It was going to be a very hot day.

What I saw before me—the white sand street, the men conversing, the weeds growing alongside the tracks—appeared timeless, as if they had been there forever. They were part of my experience, my heritage. They were the South. I had not lived in the lower South for years. I was a teacher now at a university in the North. Yet I was sure that I could walk over to where those three men were talking, enter into their conversation, and understand every word they were saying and why they were saying it.

Until then, I had never thought about it in quite that way.

Still, as I considered it some more, what I was seeing was *not* timeless. The train to Wilmington, alongside which the men were standing and talking, would

soon be leaving on its run, as would the train on which I would be traveling. It would be making its way down into South Carolina and toward Charleston. In place of the familiar little gas-electric coach that I had hoped to photograph after all these years, a Baldwin diesel-electric locomotive was waiting to make the run. Diesel locomotives, not steam, now powered the main-line passenger trains with their streamlined stainless-steel coaches that stopped at the Hamlet station en route between Florida and Atlanta and the Northeast. The soldiers and sailors in uniform that had thronged the station platform during the war were no longer in evidence.

Much that appeared unchanging was in fact changing all the time.

I went back into the day coach and sat down. As I watched, a black man, dressed in a suit and with a straw hat, walked along the aisle, through the section of the coach in which I was seating, and into the separate, segregated section. My years in Baltimore and in New Jersey made that seem strange to me—uncomfortably so. So there were also some ways in which I was no longer as one with those men who were conversing over by the vestibule of the other train.

———

Presently the conductor outside called "*All aboard!*" and train No. 25, formerly but no longer the Boll Weevil, set out for Charleston and Savannah. It clattered across the main line in front of the station. The route led southward and southeastward down through eastern South Carolina to Andrews, about forty miles from the ocean, then turned southwest and paralleled the coast line through Charleston down to Savannah. We left the outskirts of Hamlet and moved through pinelands, past farms and fields. The conductor, a middle-aged man in a shiny black suit with gold buttons, collected my ticket. Noting my destination, he remarked, "Going all the way, huh?"

I nodded. "Is that unusual?"

"It is nowadays. Didn't use to be."

At Gibson, North Carolina, near the state line, seven black men, four of them barefooted, were seated along the station platform, their legs dangling down in the sun. They were dressed in nondescript clothes and denim overalls and wore caps of many colors. To a traveler from the North they would be seen as Local Color quaintness. They probably did not have jobs.

At Clio, South Carolina, twenty-four miles down the line, there was a rickety Victorian mansion near the station, with unpainted corner towers, three-columned porch supports, tooled banisters, and frayed wooden shingles. On the back porch a rusty iron pump was mounted. The house may well have antedated the coming of the railroad; the chances of anyone building a home like that next to the tracks, even before the automobile had made it both practical and fashionable to live on the outskirts of a town, seemed slight.

The conductor and several trainmen were seated in the coach talking, and I went over and sat down across from them. "What happened to the Boll Weevil?" I asked. "I was hoping to ride it."

It turned out that the gas-electrics had been gone for two years, replaced by diesels that were especially designed for use on secondary passenger runs. Counterparts of the Boll Weevils were said to be still operating out of Savannah on the Seaboard's line to Montgomery, Alabama. The trainmen appeared to be in no way grieved at their departure from the Hamlet Division. The combines had frequently broken down on the job, necessitating repairs and often putting them behind schedule.

I said that I had heard them called Boll Weevils ever since I was a child in Charleston in the late 1920s and early 1930s. "They used to call them doodlebugs, too," the conductor told me. The name Boll Weevil was unofficial, he said. The black people who lived in the sea island country along the coast came up with it, following the advent of the bug that had wiped out the culture of long-fibered cotton during the 1910s and 1920s: "The bug was little, and the train was little, too."

He quoted dialogue. People said, "Where you goin'?"

"Goin' to Meggetts."

"How you goin' to Meggetts?"

"Goin' to ride the Boll Weevil."

"Oh."

"They used to say, 'That Boll Weevil, she run the fastest, stop the quickest, and stay the longest of any train,'" he said. It was obviously a routine he had delivered more than once, for the benefit of visitors.

At Minturn, S.C., a girl in a faded pink dress stood at the doorway of a dilapidated tobacco warehouse. Inside were piles of yellow tobacco leaves. A red jeep bounced by on a sand road. July was the season when the first tobacco crop was harvested and auctioned off at warehouses throughout this part of the Carolinas.

Another eight miles and we were at the edge of Dillon, where we crossed the Atlantic Coast Line main line. According to the Coast Line schedule the Havana Special would be passing through soon, bound for Florence and North Charleston. When I was growing up, it was always aboard the Havana Special that I had envisioned myself as one day leaving for the cities of the Northeast, and coming home from those places. And I could have done so on this trip, traveling in style aboard a fast train with club car, diners, and a long string of coaches, pulled by three diesel units, leaving Richmond in the morning and arriving in the early afternoon—just as when a child I had watched it come rolling up to the North Station behind a pair of steam locomotives. But here I was, riding along on the single day-coach successor to the little Seaboard Boll Weevil, seeing places I had not seen before, and finding out at last where the Boll Weevil went.

After a few minutes the train came to a halt, and began backing along a wye track into the Seaboard station in Dillon. We came to a stop next to a covered platform. Beyond the rear vestibule of the coach the tracks continued across what seemed to be the main street of Dillon, and on the far side and facing us was an old 4–8–2 locomotive, its snout loaded with booster pumps and tanks. Behind the tender were some box-cars and a caboose. A way freight train, it had been working along the line ahead of us, the conductor told me, and had backed onto the wye to allow us and a northbound through freight to go by. The loco-motive was suspiring lightly, and a light trail of smoke rose straight into the air. On its pilot, next to the main street, was half of a striped tiger watermelon, its innards partly consumed. A black flagman and a white engi-neer were standing next to it talking.

I went down the vestibule steps and took some photographs. We stayed at the station almost fifteen minutes. I could hear the diesel locomotives and the train of boxcars of the northbound through freight drone through town a couple of blocks off to the west. Then our train headed back down the wye and south-bound onto the tracks.

We passed through Mullins and Gresham, then crossed a trestle over the Pee Dee River. The river water was black and the banks were tangled with bram-ble and reed grass. I had read somewhere that Stephen Foster had originally written his song as "Way down upon the Pee Dee River, far far away," but had thought better of it and substituted the more euphonious "Swa-nee." We moved through a succession of towns—Pos-ton, Johnsonville, Hemingway—in country laced with swamps, creeks, and stands of cypress and oak. This was the country in which Francis Marion had operated against Cornwallis during the Revolutionary War. "A moment in the British camp— / A moment, and away / Back through the pathless forest, / Before the peep of day," as William Cullen Bryant's poem went. In the sixth grade we had to memorize it.

———

So it went. It was after 1:30 before we reached Andrews, a town of just under two thousand population. We were to be at the station for fifteen minutes, the con-ductor told me, and would wait until a bus arrived from Georgetown, down on the coast. Across the tracks was a swaybacked, unpainted building that the conductor

said was a restaurant. The front porch slanted down-ward. On it were a swing and several chairs, one of them with upholstery half burned away by fire. Inside, on a plank floor, was a room with an oil heater in the center painted an imitation wood finish, gray over-stuffed chairs, and a sofa. To the left was a long table covered with bright print oilcloth and red-and-chrome chairs arranged around it. A coffeemaker stood on a nearby wooden table with a stack of stoneware cups and saucers.

"All we got is ham," I was told by a woman who came in from the kitchen. I ordered a ham sandwich. It was packinghouse, not country cured, and was handed to me on a paper napkin. I took it back to the coach.

During the war, the conductor said, Andrews had been quite a busy place. A daily passenger train, not a bus, connected it with Georgetown, where there was a shipyard, and numerous people rode to Andrews aboard the Boll Weevil, then changed over to the Georgetown train. Andrews had been a railroad meal stop for years, he said, but not many railroad travelers patronized the restaurant any more. I could well believe it.

The Georgetown bus arrived, with two people on it. We set off down the line but soon pulled to a stop at Andrews Yard, where we moved onto a siding. We were to wait until a certain time for the northbound train, No. 26, then if it did not arrive, move on to the next stop and wait there. I went out onto the rear vestibule and down onto the ground. To the east of the tracks was a network of switching tracks, rusted and with weeds among the crossties and along the rails, and not a boxcar anywhere in sight. It was left over from the war, a brakeman standing nearby said; then it had been very busy and often loaded with freight cars.

The anvil of a thunderhead was forming in the sky above the stand of pines, to the southwest. We had left the sandhills and upstate South Carolina and were in the lowcountry, no more than twenty-five miles from the ocean. The afternoon air was hot, humid, and thick with insects. This time of year there was a thunderstorm almost every afternoon, the brakeman said. A thin young black man, he kicked between the tracks at the dried carcass of a snake. Off in the woods a bullfrog grunted.

The conductor, who had walked up to the locomotive, came ambling back. "Let's go," he said. So we climbed back into the coach, and the train moved out onto the main line, waited to pick up the brakeman, then resumed its journey. What happens, I asked the conductor, if the northbound train shows up on the line before we get to Oceda, the next stop? It won't, he explained. The arrangement was that if it did not reach Oceda by a certain time, it was to halt when it got there and wait for the southbound section to arrive.

At Oceda several black people boarded the train. We waited at the siding. Presently No. 26 came into sight, moving at a brisk clip. It clicked past us, red-and-yellow diesel, baggage car, and single day coach, and up the line, bound for Hamlet. Now we returned to the line and were off for Charleston.

The sky had grown darker, and soon the rain came, driving hard against the windows of the coach. I could see the lightning flashes, but the accompanying thunderclaps were faint, their sound masked by the air-conditioning and the running of the train. Within minutes the rain slackened; we had passed through the thunderstorm.

We were coming into the Santee River floodplain, with marshes and creeks and shaded recesses of woods draped with Spanish moss. No doubt there were alligators in the dark water, and very likely black bears in the thickets and woods. The river itself was quite wide, with a belt of marshland. Beyond it, on solid ground again, there were stretches of farmland, with black soil, then more marshes and creeks and cypress trees with knobs. We could not be too far from the area called Hell Hole Swamp, which during Prohibition days was one of the prime moonshine-distilling centers in the Southeast.

There were extensive tracts of open marsh grass and streams, with the tracks running above them along a wooden trestle. This was the upper reach of the Cooper River, which together with the Ashley formed Charleston harbor. As often as I had gone down to the Charleston waterfront and watched the ships, tugs, trawlers, and small craft, the upper Cooper was unknown territory for me. Herons and egrets were in place along the brackish marsh; here and there were duck blinds camouflaged by reed grass. I could remember, as a child, paddling along the marsh creeks on the Ashley River in a leaky wooden boat. Clouds of tiny white insects might rise up when I rounded a bend, or an occasional startled heron or marsh hen that would fly up suddenly and wing away.

But now we were moving down onto the Charleston peninsula. When a child I used to wonder where the route of the Boll Weevil led after it left the pink stucco station at the ballpark. How did it make its way through Charleston Neck and North Charleston? The path it took through the city had remained unknown to me.

Back then the little train had seemed so familiar, so ordinary, totally without surprise or mystery. Yet there were places that it went, areas it traversed that I did not know, even in Charleston itself.

We passed the Army Port of Embarkation, where in the summer of 1942 I had a job as a checker, supervising a gang of workers unloading freight cars. Then we were in North Charleston itself, crossing the main street. I had worked there as a reporter on a little weekly newspaper not a mile up the way, yet I had never noticed that the Seaboard tracks passed by. Now we were rolling past the Navy Yard, where my father would take us on Sundays sometimes during my childhood to play aboard the wooden hill of Admiral Farragut's old flagship at Mobile Bay, the *Hartford*. The Cooper River Bridge was in sight, with its double arches spanning the harbor. We were in the rail yards at Cherokee. Soon we were moving through Magnolia Crossing, curving past the junior high school.

So this was where the Boll Weevil went when it left the ballpark!

———

Train No. 25, successor to the Boll Weevil, slowed to a crawl as it moved through the intersection at King Street and came along Grove to Rutledge Avenue, where the crossing barriers came down and the alarm bell sounded. It passed by the grandstand at College Park and came to a stop at the station.

I lifted my suitcase down from the overhead rack, stepping along the aisle and out into the vestibule and down onto the concrete walk alongside the track. I walked through the baseball parking lot over to Rutledge Avenue, crossed Grove Street, and waited for a downtown bus.

An odd thing happened then. A boy came wheeling along the sidewalk on a bicycle, a baseball glove looped through the handlebars. I recognized him and started to say his name: "Billy!" Then I realized that this was a much younger boy who happened to look something like a boy I had known ten years earlier, for the Billy I remembered would be a grown man in his middle twenties.

The Rutledge Avenue bus came along, and I got aboard and headed downtown to my aunt's. That was in July of 1950. A week later I went back to Baltimore on the Havana Special. In early September the school year began. That fall I met the girl who would become my wife.

———

Why, after all these years, is this six-hour train trip so memorable for me?

When I was growing up, I had thought of trains in terms of leaving for distant places and to new experiences. But when I made that trip from Hamlet to Charleston, I was coming to see that it was in the rediscovery of what I had once believed ordinary and commonplace that as a writer and teacher of writers I would be working. Not only the express trains, but the little Boll Weevil, meandering through terrain that I thought I knew by heart, could bear me where I wanted to go. The trip I took that day was not only a ride on a train, but the journey into a vocation.

Nine Marcel Proust and the Seaboard Coast Line

Casey said before he died
There's two more roads that I wanted to ride
The fireman asked him what could they be
He said, The Southern Pacific and the MKT
                                    —song, "Casey Jones"

If this book were about myself as such, instead of about the trains that I remember, it might well have ended with that six-hour trip down to Charleston. But there were many more trains and railroads to see and ride.

To begin with, my longtime ambition to travel beyond the mountains and to have a look at Midwestern railroading was finally achieved. After our marriage in 1951, my wife and I drove out to Cincinnati, my wife's home. We stayed overnight in Washington Court House, Ohio, and in the morning I stopped by the railroad station and found an especially imposing 2–8–2 Mikado about to come through at the head of a Detroit, Toledo, and Ironton freight train. The DT&I, which Henry Ford had founded, ran from the edge of the coal country at the Ohio River through Springfield and Toledo, Ohio, to Detroit and the Great Lakes.

In Cincinnati I spent a morning at the suburban station at Winton Place, through which the New York Central, Pennsylvania, Baltimore and Ohio, and Norfolk and Western were all operating trains. Assorted NYC steam locomotives were in evidence, but mainly it was diesel.

With my wife's parents we drove out for her sister's wedding in Madison, Wisconsin. There I found a splendid little Milwaukee Road 0–6–0 with high domes

puffing its way up and down the lakefront, spotting hopper cars. The handwriting was on the roundhouse wall for steam in those parts, too; a Chicago and Northwestern diesel streamliner came cruising serenely by as I watched. On the way back, somewhere in Illinois, I photographed a Milwaukee Road freight train with an Electro-Motive diesel flying white extra flags at the head. Between Madison and Cincinnati we did not encounter a single steam locomotive.

On the way home from Cincinnati, we took an unscheduled and unwanted train ride. Shortly after we left Uniontown, Pennsylvania, our old 1941 Pontiac reached the top of a steep hill, whereupon, as if celebrating the successful ascent, the transmission began to clank like a job printing press. I put the gear into neutral and we coasted down a long slope and up to the open doors of a garage fortuitously located at the base of the hill. On the wall of the garage was a poster proclaiming, Pontiac: The 100,000-Mile Engine. The odometer on our car read just over 100,300 miles. Talk about Truth in Advertising!

We left the car there, flagged down a bus, and rode to Cumberland, Maryland, and after a three-hour wait in the passenger station there, returned to Baltimore aboard the B&O. A week later I rode the B&O back to Cumberland and took a Greyhound bus back to the garage near Uniontown. The mechanic had doctored the transmission sufficiently to allow me to get safely back to Baltimore, he said, but his earnest advice was to trade it in on another car once I got home.

Another trip on the B&O was decidedly more gratifying. I was invited to lecture at a writers' conference at the University of Missouri, and I rode out to Chicago on a B&O train with a dome car. Because of tunnel clearances the dome was lower than those on the western trains, but the panoramic midnight view of the steel mills near Pittsburgh, flaring orange and yellow against the sky, was superb. From Chicago I took the Alton down to St. Louis and the Wabash to Centralia, Missouri. Everything was diesel-powered. The Wabash's streamlined City of St. Louis was a beautiful train, but I had the lounge car all to myself. As was true almost everywhere except along the Northeast Corridor between New York and Washington, passenger travel was tailing off swiftly, and not even the streamliner's comfort and speed—it averaged 56 miles an hour between St. Louis and Kansas City—could fend off the decline.

I had a chance to ride on the highest main-line railroad trackage east of the Rockies—in an automobile. The *Baltimore Sun*, for whose Sunday magazine I occasionally wrote, asked me to accompany the newspaper's star photographer, Aubrey Bodine, to write a feature story on a branch of the Western Maryland Railroad. We drove to Cumberland, Maryland, and were then driven to Elkins, West Virginia. There we got into a station wagon that had been equipped with flanged wheels and a pilot out front, for operation on the rails, and set off up the track. There was a mixed train—passenger and freight—that ran daily between Elkins and Durbin, forty-seven miles away, but it operated at night, which would not do for taking photographs.

We proceeded to the Western Maryland's hunting lodge, which was well up in the mountains and accessible only by rail. We were the sole guests. A luxurious affair, it was designed for use by the road's executives and their customers. There were registers going back before the turn of the century, with entries for

expeditions in which hordes of deer and bear were proudly recorded as having been shot by visiting sportsmen. The lodge maintained a pond stocked with trout; fly-fishing equipment was provided, including trout flies with barbless hooks. Almost every cast produced a good-sized rainbow trout. After taking and releasing three or four I had had enough. Later I saw the custodian of the lodge down in a glen behind the building, casting for wild brookies in a stream. The chances of taking one were very slim, he said, but at least some skill and luck were involved.

In the morning we went out very early, to allow the photographer to take advantage of mist and shadows. The mountain scenery along the line was magnificent, with rocky cliffsides, precipitous dropoffs, and winding curves. We visited coal tipples, mine entrances, and remote stations and yards. From the standpoint of photographing trains as such, however, the prospects were poor, for the single freight train that traversed the line during the day, pulling a string of hopper cars, was powered by three look-alike road-switcher diesels, black and not very photogenic. On a mountainside, far above us, I could see the smoke of a logging train, very likely powered by a wood-burning Shay or Heisler locomotive, but nowhere close to being accessible from where we were.

Later that summer, however, I did see a Heisler at work up close. My wife and I were driving east from Cincinnati, and after visiting friends in Kentucky we started across the West Virginia mountains on U.S. 50. We drove through a town named Rupert. There was a railroad crossing ahead, and as we drew near I heard a high-pitched whistle. I pulled off the highway, picked up my camera, and took up position alongside the tracks, which were narrow-gauge. Another whistle, this time close by, then several open flatcars came around a sharp curve, one of them bearing a bulldozer, then a gondola car, and, pushing from the rear, a locomotive with a bell stack and the pistons working at a 45-degree angle rather than horizontally for maximum tractive effort on steep mountain grades. Along its side was the name Meadow River Lumber Company. I was so excited that neither of the shots I made was in precise focus, and thus I failed to make full use of the only chance I would ever have to photograph a working, non–tourist-trade, wood-burning locomotive.

———

If I had seen Midwestern roads, I had yet to have a look at true transcontinental railroading. But in 1954 I took a job that, for someone who enjoyed riding on trains, was made to order. That June I received my doctorate, but because of intra-university politics at Johns Hopkins there was no possibility either of my being promoted or given a raise in salary there. So when I was offered a position as executive secretary of a scholarly society, the American Studies Association, which had just received a three-year developmental grant from the Carnegie Corporation, I accepted it at once. It carried with it an assistant professorship of American Civilization at the University of Pennsylvania, though I would teach no classes.

The Association, made up of scholars in various academic fields who were specialists in American civilization, was organized regionally, with groups in the process of formation throughout the United States. It would be my responsibility to work with the scholars who were setting up the regional groups—which meant visiting them and attending their organizational meetings.

What it came down to was that I now had a legitimate reason to ride on trains throughout the United States, with my full expenses covered.

We moved to suburban Philadelphia in July, and that fall I made my first expedition, to meet with groups in Los Angeles and San Francisco, with stopoffs along the way. With its numerous segments, the round-trip ticket was more than a yard long.

Steam locomotives were in ever shorter supply. It was not until I found myself at Hammond, Louisiana, waiting for friends to come and take me to Baton Rouge, that I photographed an Illinois Central long

freight train pulled by a 2–8–2 Mikado coming through, and an elderly 4–6–2 Pacific spotting freight cars. Otherwise it was diesels from Cincinnati to New Orleans. From New Orleans I would take the Sunset Limited to the West Coast, with a stop in El Paso and a side trip to Albuquerque, and I looked forward to seeing the famous oil-burning 4–8–8–2 Mallets of the Southern Pacific, with their cabs located at the head of the train for better vision around mountain curves. But they were all gone, replaced by diesels several months earlier. Not only that, but to make sure that the decision would not be reversed, the operating authorities on the SP's New Orleans-to-Los Angeles run had dismantled all the water tanks en route, rendering steam railroading impossible.

The Sunset Limited left New Orleans shortly before midnight, and it arrived in El Paso a little more than twenty-four hours later. The route led due westward across southern Texas, through Houston and San Antonio, to Del Rio, on the U.S.-Texas border at the Rio Grande, 743 miles away. We arrived there in mid-afternoon. From there the long train with its three road diesel units at the head end climbed northwestward through largely uninhabited country that became increasingly mountainous as we went. During the 310 miles to El Paso there were exactly five stops, and of those only Sanderson, population 2,500, was of consequence. As long as there was daylight to see by, the journey was interesting. It was the roughest, most inhospitable terrain I had ever seen, with only an occasional road along winding defiles, and a ranch house and barn a rare sight.

I remembered Carl Sandburg's poem, "Slabs of the Sunburnt West"; sunburnt, yes, but scarcely slabs—rather, humps, knobs, aretes, spines, spurs, peaks, ridges. By the time we reached Alpine, Texas, with mountains six thousand feet high or more, it was turning dark, and soon thereafter we were riding through the night, with the blackness beyond the Pullman's roomette windows only interrupted at extended intervals by a far-off light or two. It was 11:30 P.M. when we arrived at El Paso. That was the only time that I could ever remember being totally bored while traveling on a railroad train.

In El Paso I visited with an uncle for several days, flew up to Albuquerque and back, then continued on to Los Angeles aboard the Sunset Limited, and up the coast to San Francisco. At one point I did see steam locomotives on the Southern Pacific: several 4–6–2 Pacifics with bright silver smoke-box fronts were pulling local trains between San Jose and San Francisco. Otherwise it was all diesel.

On the Union Pacific eastward from Oakland I enjoyed a well-prepared medium-rare steak aboard a dining car named the Golden Nugget. There was only one other patron in the car. The next morning we were crossing the Great Salt Lake when I woke up, and from my roomette window all I could see was very blue water. That day I looked for Big Boys, the UP 4–8–8–4s that were reputedly the largest and most powerful Mallets in the world. Not a Big Boy did I see. From Laramie, Wyoming, I had a fine ride in a dome car on the diesel-powered City of San Francisco, watching the needle on the speedometer reach and pass eighty miles an hour as we streaked eastward.

Two days later, from Iowa City to Chicago I rode aboard another dome car on the Des Moines Rocket. At Rock Island I watched the crossing of the Mississippi River; it was a stunning view. Across the Illinois prairie the train was also doing well over seventy. "If you want / to ride it / you must ride it / where you find it / get your ticket / at the station / on the Rock Island Line." Along the way a few steam locomotives were working freight drags here and there along the way, but the diesels were handling all the through trains.

This was the experience of railroading I had always wanted to see. There was another poem by Carl Sandburg, titled "Limited," that I had read and admired very much:

I am riding on a limited express, one of the crack trains of the nation.

Hurtling across the prairie into blue haze and dark air go fifteen all-steel coaches holding a thousand people.
(All the coaches shall be scrap and rust and all the men and women laughing in the diners and sleepers shall pass to ashes.)
I ask a man in the smoker where he is going and he answers: "Omaha."

Now I was aboard just such a train, hurtling across the prairie, as the poem had it, along tracks straight as a drawn line for hundreds of miles, unslowed by steep grades and tunnels. Yet the trains, the ultimate in transcontinental railroading, powered by shiny diesel-electric road locomotives and with modern, comfortable equipment and excellent dining car service, had few riders.

On another western excursion, en route to a meeting in Greeley, Colorado, I had an appointment in St. Louis. I had read that more railroads used the St. Louis Union Station than any other in the country, and I arranged to go out to the head of the station tracks and photograph trains. I spent two hours there, taking photos of the passenger trains of railroads I had never seen until then—the Frisco Line, the Gulf Mobile and Ohio, the Katy, the Missouri Pacific, the St. Louis Southwestern, the Burlington. All were diesel-powered, every last one of them, and their galaxy of colors could not translate very well into black-and-white.

Yet when I left Kansas City for Denver it was aboard a Pullman at the rear of a Union Pacific train with a 4–8–4 Northern at the head end. We sped across Kansas leaving a trail of smoke to drift over the prairie in the best old-style railroading form. In the morning when we arrived at Denver I was not due at Greeley for my meeting until the evening, so I rented a car and drove southward along the Denver and Rio Grande Western trackage, where I saw a Burlington Route Mikado put up a fine plume of smoke as it pulled a freight train, with the Rocky Mountains for backdrop.

When the meetings at Greeley were over I rode up to Cheyenne, Wyoming, to take a train to Chicago. It was late afternoon, and Cheyenne looked more like a Wild West town than any place I had yet seen; I expected a posse to come riding down the main street. Along one side of the UP yards was a melancholy sight: two tracks lined with steam locomotives in various stages of dismantlement, including everything from articulated Mallets to switch engines. At their head was a ten-wheeler with a wide cab, ornate domes, a handsome bell, and a high stack with a spark arrester atop it; at the very latest it must have dated from the early 1900s.*

They were waiting to become scrap and ashes, as in the poem. The Iron Horse was vanishing from the UP Trail. I took some photographs while there was still some light left, then waited at the passenger station for the eastbound diesel-powered streamliner that would take me to Chicago.

For a meeting in East Lansing, Michigan, my wife and I drove from Philadelphia to Hamilton, Ontario, and westward across the peninsula. I had hoped to see steam locomotives in Canada, and I was not disappointed. At Hamilton the Canadian National had an 0–6–0 moving boxcars around, and a spic-and-span 2–8–0 Consolidation came through town pulling a freight train. On a siding near London, Ontario, a Canadian Pacific 2–8–2 Mikado waited on a siding with a long freight drag. We crossed back over to the United States at Port Huron, Michigan. At Lansing I stopped by a Grand Trunk Western station—as I child I had read how the young Thomas Alva Edison had worked as a news butcher on the Grand Trunk Western. After a while a freight train moved by. It was pow-

ered by two road-switcher diesels. Down the line I could see a steam locomotive, but it came no nearer.

After the meeting we drove down to Cincinnati along U.S. 127, one of those surveyed-into-place Midwestern roads that led almost in a straight line for hundreds of miles. South of Bryan, Ohio, as we drove through a crossing, the alarm bell began sounding. My wife still tells of how swiftly I pulled over to the roadside beyond the crossing and got outside the car with my camera that day. There was black smoke close by. A New York Central 2–8–2 Mikado came barreling along at the head of a freight train, drive wheels rolling and pistons churning, making a mile a minute. I was standing so close to it that I could not even get the tender into my photograph.

That was in 1954. By then relatively few steam locomotives remained in active main-line railroad service anywhere. Even the Chesapeake and Ohio, which only a few years earlier had developed the steam-turbine 500's to prove that the coal the road carried was capable of holding off the diesels, had capitulated. Yellow-and-blue Electro-Motive road units now pulled not only the passenger trains but even the long coal drags from Clifton Forge to Richmond to the sea. Eventually, of the major roads only the Norfolk and Western Railway still held out.

———

As luck would have it, when the finale of the Iron Horse came I was in the right place to watch. In 1957 I became a member of the faculty of Hollins College, near Roanoke, Virginia. That year diesel locomotives were doing 96 percent of the switching, 93 percent of the passenger carrying, and 92 percent of the freight hauling on American railroads. In the words of the railroad historian John C. Stover, "the lonesome sound of the steam whistle that had meant so much to generations of Americans had given way to the raw bleat of the diesel horn."

Roanoke was the headquarters of the Norfolk and Western. The N&W built its own steam locomotives.

---

* Recently I learned that this was the famous UP No. 1242, built by Crook Locomotive Works of Paterson, New Jersey, in 1890, which operated until 1954, and nowadays is being restored and is on display in Laramie.

From the shops at Roanoke came the 2–6–6–4's, the Y6 2–8–8–2's, and the J-class 4–8–4s, the world's most powerful Northerns. The president of the N&W, R. H. Smith, who was a member of the Hollins College board of trustees, had come up through the operations ranks. For as long as he was head of the railroad, there would be no running of road diesels on its rails. No sirree. When the Southern Railway's Tennessean and Birmingham Special arrived in Lynchburg to enter N&W trackage, J-class steam locomotives were hooked up to the green-and-white Southern diesels to pull them along the 200-mile run to Bristol, Virginia-Tennessee. It was an odd sight to see one of them moving past the Roanoke station: the working steam locomotive with the deadheaded diesels and the consist of three or four coaches that by the late 1950s were what still remained of those once-magnificent stream-lined trains.

Then R. H. Smith retired, and an attorney without an operations background, Stuart Saunders, succeeded to the presidency of the N&W. As a young man Saunders had never peered out of the window of a steam locomotive or grasped a Johnson bar. Forthwith the decision was made. In 1959 the Norfolk and Western Railway placed orders for Electromotive road diesels. Sic transit Gloria Swanson.

I commissioned an artist friend of mine to do a painting of a Mallet before they were all gone. We drove over to Bonsack, Virginia, and photographed some Y-6's as they came rumbling through with coal trains. The painting he produced, however, turned out to be of a hybrid 2–6–6–2 down at the Roanoke shops, and since Artistic Integrity made it taboo to depict anything without altering it, he messed around some with the details. Even so, I like to think that the locomotive is the same one that I saw late one evening in the summer of 1948, when a girlfriend and I were seated in my little Plymouth coupe at a grade crossing at Elkton, Virginia, waiting for a train to come through. Out of the darkness of the Shenandoah Valley, at full tilt a 2–6–6–2 Mallet shot past the intersection, a train of boxcars in tow. Freight train or not, it was moving through the night at a good sixty miles an hour. It was the single most dramatic railroading moment I have ever known.

Soon the Y-6's were running only at the head of extras, and not long after that all the N&W steam locomotives were gone. The last time I drove my son over to Bonsack to watch trains in the mid-1960s all that we saw were two groups of five diesel road-switchers pulling coal trains eastward.

A few of the steam giants have been preserved in museums and occasionally take to the rails for excursions. My son, working as a reporter on the *Roanoke Times-World* in the 1980s, rode behind a J-class 4–8–4 on a railfan excursion to Hampton Roads. One of the pilot truck wheels slipped off the rails in the Norfolk yards because it was too lengthy to negotiate a bend in the trackage.

———

In 1964, in Italy on sabbatical leave, we drove down the peninsula to Sicily. At Reggio Calabria we waited for the next ferry across to Messina. The railroad tracks were close by. Along came a steam locomotive, pushing several freight cars. Watching it, I realized that it was the first I had seen in some time.

That was the last regularly working, non–tourist-trade steam locomotive I have ever encountered. The only ones that I see now are in dreams. I will be driving alongside a track on, say, the Southern Railway, and a 2–8–2 Mikado will come along, pulling a freight train. I remind myself that all such are supposed to have been taken off the line some time ago. Yet unaccountably one is still in use. I must get my camera and take some photos, I tell myself.

They are always in black-and-white. It is pure wish-fulfillment.

———

I close this memoir of trains on a literary note. One of the three or four greatest works of literature of the twentieth century is Marcel Proust's *Remembrance of Things Past*. Early in the seven-volume novel, when the narrator and his family go walking, they have their choice of either Swann's Way or the Guermantes Way. Swann's Way goes past the estate of the stockbroker and art collector Charles Swann, who with his friends comes to symbolize the bourgeoisie, with its interest in literature and the arts. The Guermantes Way leads past the estate of one of the old aristocratic French families, the Guermantes, with their background in the history of the *ancien regime*, martial valor, and the rites of High Society.

To the young narrator these two Ways seem utterly separate and inviolable, as if permanently decreed, immune to time and change. Yet near the end of the novel the narrator, now an elderly man, attends a reception and is there introduced to a young girl. Her mother was Gilberte Swann, the daughter of Charles Swann; her father was Robert de Saint Loup, a member of the Guermantes family. Radiant in her beauty, the young girl is thus the fusion of those two Ways that to the young narrator had appeared to be so totally discrete and eternally shut off from each other. In his eyes she is symbol and proof of change and mutability.

In 1967 I picked up the morning newspaper and read that the Seaboard Air Line and the Atlantic Coast Line railroads were soon to merge into a single entity, to be called the Seaboard Coast Line. I was shocked. The route of the little gas-electric Boll Wee-vil that stopped by the ball park, and that of the triple-ballasted, double-tracked New York-to-Florida line on which the Havana Special and the other double-headed express trains that touched only briefly at North Charleston—that these roads could ever become one and the same was astounding.

Growing up as I did in a small Southern city remote from the salons, landed estates, and cosmopolitan social and cultural life of Marcel Proust's France of the late nineteenth century, railroads and the coming and going of their trains held for me the kind of

imaginative significance that Swann's Way and the Guermantes Way did for the young Marcel Proust. The realization that they were to be made into a single railroad came with a jolt.

Of course I knew very well that the Seaboard's Charleston branch had not been its main line, and that equally with the Coast Line the Seaboard had its name trains with strings of Pullmans and dining cars. Yet the emotional and imaginative assumptions of our younger days, emended and superseded though they are by our adult knowledge and experience, do not ever totally leave us. It took only that headline in a newspaper, and the associations stirred up in my memory by those two railroad names, to rekindle in my imagination the perspectives of my childhood world, when any such union would have seemed fantastic and impossible.

By the time of the merger not only the Boll Weevil but the Baldwin diesels that replaced the gas-electric combine had long since disappeared, for within a few years of my ride from Hamlet to Charleston in 1950 all passenger service had been discontinued over that route. Nor did the steam locomotives that had hauled the red-ball fruit expresses from Florida to the Northeast whistle mournfully for grade crossings off across the Ashley River any longer, for both the Seaboard and the Coast Line were fully dieselized, and had been since the mid-1950s.

Once the two roads merged there was no further need for northbound freights to use the Seaboard's branch through Charleston; the ACL's main line through North Charleston was available for all north-south freight. So the old Seaboard trackage between Charleston and Savannah was taken up and the wooden trestle over the Ashley River dismantled. Only someone who knew that trains once used to operate on tracks along Hampton Park in Charleston would understand why the grassy area at the northwest corner opens up as it does. The Seaboard's main-line trackage from Raleigh to Richmond, which I had viewed from the cab of the Silver Meteor en route to Hamlet that night in 1950, has also been scrapped. Trains now detour from Raleigh over to the old Coast Line trackage at Selma, and proceed north from there.

More than that, the Seaboard Coast Line has since merged with the Chessie System, itself a product of the merger of the Chesapeake and Ohio and the Baltimore and Ohio. Together with various other roads, they are now CSX—standing for Chesapeake Seaboard Expanded. As for the Southern Railway of my childhood, with the high-wheeled green engines trimmed in silver, it has become part of the Norfolk Southern, along with the Norfolk and Western, the Virginian, and other roads. All passenger service is handled by Amtrak now.

So the three railroads that bounded my life as a child growing up in Charleston, each with its different look and personality, no longer exist in the forms they once assumed. Like the two Ways of Marcel Proust's novel, they had only seemed to be separate and permanent; they were in fact changing all the time, were themselves the agency of change.

———

I am sure that there are those who, reading what I have written about trains, will find it inexplicable that anyone could ever have attached so much imaginative importance to the coming and going of mechanical objects designed to facilitate travel and the commercial exchange of commodities. About such things there can be no rational argument. I can only reply that in viewing locomotives and trains as possessing an importance beyond that of mere usefulness, I was not alone.

I can remember, as a youth, going with my uncle on a bicycle expedition through the country around Charleston. We spent the night at Walterboro, South Carolina, and the next day rode on to the town of St. George, arriving there in midafternoon. The Southern Railway station was not far away from our hotel, and late in the afternoon a sizeable crowd gathered there. I walked over to watch. Presently there was the hooting of a whistle to the east of town, and a high-wheeled green-and-silver 4–6–2 locomotive puffed into view, coming to a halt alongside the station and facing the main street. Passengers got off and on the coaches. Baggage and mail were unloaded and taken on. Then the "*All aboard!*" came, the air brakes went off, and the train resumed its journey, crossing the main street and soon disappearing from sight, leaving a trail of coal smoke over the downtown rooftops.

Why were all those people there at the station? Some, of course, were legitimately present on errands—to see relatives and friends off, to welcome them home, to collect packages arriving via Railway Express. Others, however, had no logical reason to be at the station. They were there to watch No. 11 come in from Charleston, forty-six miles away, to see who got off the train and who went aboard it—to view, and to take part in, the spectacle: the advent of the evening train.

They were there to watch the world come in. And so was I.

Pacific locomotives in first-class condition pull an Atlantic Coast Line
mail and railway express train southbound from Broad Street Station,
Richmond, Virginia, in February 1947. Until the coming of the
diesels, doubleheaded 4–6–2 locomotives like these were often at
the head of the ACL's crack passenger trains.

A northbound Atlantic Coast Line freight train, running extra behind
a 4–6–2 Pacific, moves through Petersburg, Virginia, May 1948.

Hear that lonesome whistle. Johnny Mercer was from Savannah, but
if it were nighttime and the windows were open, and if you lived in
Richmond and heard an Atlantic Coast Line freight train like this
blowing across the James River trestle with a load of empty refrigerator cars, you would get the idea. May 1948.

The Havana Special, my own paragon among trains when young,
makes a scheduled stop in downtown Rocky Mount, North Carolina,
where the tracks ran down the middle of the main street, to change
crews. This was in February of 1947, when it was pulled by a silver-
and-purple EMD E-7. Rocky Mount was a major Atlantic Coast
Line division point between Richmond and Jacksonville.

The diesels were handling most Coast Line main-line freight by the late 1940s. Behind Electro-Motive diesel power this train rolls through Petersburg, Virginia, in May 1948.

A 4–6–2 Pacific heads south toward the James River viaduct with
a train of empty refrigerator cars, flying the white flags of a non-
scheduled ACL extra, in May 1948.

Doubleheaded Coast Line Pacifics roll across the trestle over the Appomattox River at Petersburg, Virginia, in May 1948, en route to the Carolinas with a freight train.

I found and photographed ACL locomotive No. 149, a 1906
Baldwin 0–6–0 switch engine, on a track next to the Union Station
in Charleston, South Carolina, in February 1947, waiting for a ride
to the boneyard. Its diminutive size, useful for negotiating spur tracks
to warehouses and wharves, probably kept it in service during the
war years.

A rare photograph of the Atlantic Coast Line's Vacationer, taken in late December of 1946, not long after its reinstatement following wartime suspension. It is arriving in Richmond from the South and en route to Broad Street Station, behind EMD diesels.

This is the first locomotive photograph I ever took. A Seaboard Mikado-type (2–8–2) freight locomotive waits at the Seaboard Air Line's Hermitage yards in Richmond for its next assignment, September 7, 1946.

70

The once and future king: a Seaboard Electro-Motive road
unit at Hermitage Yards, Richmond, September 7, 1946.

Workhorses of the Seaboard for many years, doubleheaded Mikado
2–8–2s are hauling a long train of refrigerated fruit from Florida into
Hermitage Yards, Richmond, in November 1947. Throughout my
childhood I heard these northbound steam locomotives rumbling
across the wooden trestle over the Ashley River in Charleston, and
wondered why almost no southbound freights ever came through.

EMD diesels convey a Seaboard refrigerator car train across the Appomattox River at Petersburg, May 1947. The tracks along the riverbank are the Norfolk and Western's.

A Seaboard 4–8–2 Mountain-type locomotive, its days of mainline service numbered, brings a passenger local into Petersburg, Virginia, in May 1948.

The Boll Weevil—gas-electric doodlebug and single passenger coach—
stopping at Charleston, perhaps at the Seaboard yards near Cherokee,
sometime in the 1930s. Trains No. 25 and 26 operated daily along the
South Carolina coast between Savannah, Georgia, and Hamlet, across
the North Carolina state line. The name itself was informal, applied by
its sea island clientele. This is the only photograph in this book not
made by me.

Baldwin diesel-electric locomotive No. 2702, successor to the Boll
Weevil, and its train, and a 4–8–2 Mountain steam locomotive with
another Seaboard local in position at Hamlet, North Carolina, in July
of 1950, ready to leave for Savannah and for Wilmington.

Right: The Wilmington local and the oddly roofed Seaboard station
in Hamlet, July 1950. Five years earlier and this scene would have
included men in military uniform. The Seaboard's main line southbound traffic from Richmond diverged here for Florida and for
Atlanta and Birmingham.

This view of Seaboard Baldwin diesel No. 2702, with baggage car and day coach, is at Andrews, South Carolina, in July 1950. The SAL's three small Baldwin diesels were known as "Babyfaces."

A Seaboard 4–8–2 Mountain locomotive, relegated to working a way freight along the Hamlet, Charleston, and Savannah branch, has backed onto a wye at Dillon, South Carolina, to enable passenger train No. 25 and a northbound through freight to come through. The object lying on the pilot next to the flagman and the engineer is a partly consumed watermelon. July 1950.

EMD diesels haul northbound Seaboard Air Line passenger train No. 4 into Hermitage Yards, Richmond, in December 1946.

Right: A priority southbound freight train, hauling refrigerator car empties with a three-unit Seaboard EMD diesel in front, cruises into Petersburg, Virginia, in May 1948. Note the steam switch engine on the sidetrack.

A green-and-silver 4–6–2 Pacific locomotive powers the Southern
Railway's Carolina Special near Five Points in Columbia, South
Carolina, in February 1947.

One of the Southern Railway's classic high-wheel 4–6–2 Pacifics
waits at Hull Street Station, South Richmond, Virginia, to make the
afternoon trip to Danville, in 1948. Within two years a diesel road-
switcher would be assigned to the run. It was on this line that Jefferson Davis and the Confederate cabinet had fled from Richmond when
Grant's army broke through the defenses at Petersburg in April 1865.

The workhorse of the Southern Railway: a 2–8–2 Mikado freight locomotive at the Charleston roundhouse, in February 1947. From New Orleans to Norfolk, Southern Mikes hauled much of the freight for several generations. As the augmented slogan went, "The Southern Serves the South—and It Serves It Right."

Another Southern Mike 2–8–2 pulls a way freight south of
Charlottesville, Virginia, bound for the Monroe yards near
Lynchburg in July of 1947.

Still another well-groomed Southern 2–8–2 Mikado at the yards
in South Richmond. February 1947.

It is autumn 1953, the green-and-silver Pacifics that used to pull the Southern passenger trains have gone, and an EMD diesel-electric brings the Royal Palm past the big hook and into the station at Lexington, Kentucky, en route to Chattanooga and Atlanta.

The Governor Braxton, a 4–8–4 Northern, is conducting a
Richmond, Fredericksburg and Potomac local into Broad Street
Station in Richmond, in May of 1947.

A long RF&P train of freight cars comes through the C&O crossing at Doswell, Virginia, from Potomac yards at Alexandria and bound for Acca yards in Richmond, pulled by a 2–8–4 Berkshire locomotive.

An RF&P work train, with big hook and crew quarters, arrives
at Doswell, Virginia, where the Chesapeake and Ohio tracks cross.
The locomotive is a 4–6–2 Pacific. April 1948.

A track maintenance crew lowers equipment into position to do
some grading at Doswell. April 1948.

Again at Doswell, a local RF&P freight train powered by a 4–6–2 Pacific eases past coaches used for work crew quarters. The partially buried track sections are spares for the C&O-RF&P crossing. April 1947.

Southbound 2–8–4 and freight train at Greendale, Virginia, on the
RF&P double-tracked main line, November 1947.

Hurry, hurry, hurry! You don't want to miss it! A carnival train pulled
by a 4–6–2 RF&P Pacific rolls southward through Doswell, Virginia,
in April 1948, with the gaudily painted flatcars and paraphernalia of
the Johnny J. Jones Expositions—a familiar sight at state fairs, carni-
vals, and other outdoor events.

Beauty and the beast? On the left is Norfolk and Western's steam passenger locomotive No. 122, a lovely streamlined 4–8–2, jet black with red and silver trim; on the right, one of the Richmond, Fredericksburg and Potomac EMD diesel-electrics then engaged in displacing the RF&P's stable of 4–8–4's and 2–8–4's. Broad Street Station, Richmond, mid-1950s.

An Erie 2–8–2 Mikado, blasting away at full power, leaves the yards at
Secaucus, New Jersey, with a freight train, bound for Port Jervis, New
York. January 1947.

96

Still on commuter service in Bergen County, New Jersey, in the
post–World War II years were some beautiful high-wheeled steam
locomotives dating back to the turn of the century. This Northern
Railroad of New Jersey light Pacific (4–6–2), owned by the Erie, is
pulling three coaches into North Bergen, New Jersey, late in 1946.

This Erie Railroad gas-electric with two commuter coaches in tow is arriving at Rutherford, New Jersey, from the Jersey City terminal in early 1947.

A 4–8–2 Mohawk at the head of a freight train on the New York
Central's West Shore Division at West Englewood, New Jersey,
bound for Schenectady, in January 1947.

This New York Central 4–6–4 Hudson is emerging from the tunnel under the Palisades from the Weehawken yards at North Bergen, New Jersey, with a northbound train in January 1947.

A 4–8–2 Mohawk and a through freight train barrel through Teaneck
on the New York Central's West Shore Division, headed up the Hudson
River in October 1946.

The locomotive crew are checking the journal box on the tender
of a 4–6–4 Hudson at the New York Central yards at Weehawken,
New Jersey, in December 1946.

Back Door to Broadway. The New York Central ferryboat terminal at the foot of 42nd Street, New York City, on the Hudson River opposite Weehawken in October 1946.

This New York Central 2–8–2 Mikado was making sixty-plus miles an hour with a freight train south of Bryan, Ohio, when I photographed it in September 1954. I did not even have time to move far enough away from the crossing to get the tender into the picture.

The commutation coach of the New York, Susquehanna and Western arrives at Hackensack, New Jersey, from Paterson on a Saturday morning in February 1947. Its route terminated at Susquehanna Transfer, near the entrance to the Lincoln Tunnel, where passengers would then board buses to cross under the river to downtown Manhattan.

Seen from the rear vestibule of a passing commuter train, two
Delaware, Lackawanna and Hudson steam locomotives await action
not far from the Lackawanna terminal at Hoboken, New Jersey, in
January of 1947. The locomotive on the right is a 4–8–4 Pocono,
engineered to handle long trains such as the Phoebe Snow through
the Delaware Water Gap; that on the left is probably a 4–6–2.

The Jersey Central, which specialized in camelback locomotives burning anthracite coal, used a fleet of them to pull commuter trains to and from its Jersey City terminal, but this particular 2–6–0 was engaged in shifting coaches at Allentown, Pennsylvania, in the summer of 1949.

108

The plume of bituminous smoke is thick and black as a Chesapeake and Ohio 2–8–4 Kanawha, having come down onto the Norfolk and Western Shenandoah Division tracks at Waynesboro, Virginia, exchanges some freight cars with the N&W before resuming its way freight run on its own trackage. December 1947.

Left: C&O train No. 5, the Sportsman, pulls into the upper-level platform of the Waynesboro, Virginia, station under a cloudy sky, with the Blue Ridge as backdrop, in December 1947.

At the C&O roundhouse at Clifton Forge, with the high mountains
for a backdrop, a 4–8–2 Mountain-type locomotive is in the process of
being turned. June 1947.

Clifton Forge, Virginia, was the junction point for the James River, Mountain and Kanawha Divisions of the Chesapeake and Ohio Railway. A 2–8–4 Kanawha and a 4–6–2 Pacific, with steam up, await assignments on a Sunday in June of 1947.

One of the C&O's new H-8 compound articulated 2–6–6–6 Mallets,
built to haul long trains of hopper cars up steep grades, is back to back
with a 4–8–4 Greenbrier at the Clifton Forge, Virginia, yards in June
of 1947.

With a 2–8–4 Berkshire at the head, a Chesapeake and Ohio local
passenger train winds eastward through the Blue Ridge Mountains
near Afton, Virginia, in March of 1947.

A C&O local, pulled by a 2–8–4 Kanawha locomotive, has just arrived in Charlottesville, Virginia, exactly one hour behind scheduled arrival time. 1947.

Its smoke box nicely gusseted up with booster tanks, pumps and valves, a C&O 4–8–2 Mountain-type locomotive backs into place at the Charlottesville Union Station in May of 1947 to hook onto and haul the Richmond-Newport News section of the Sportsman eastward.

This photograph, made from a hillside near Glasgow, Virginia, in October 1947, shows a long C&O freight train (right) climbing westward through the James River Gap in the Blue Ridge, while the approaching train of hopper cars is eastbound for Lynchburg, Richmond, and the wharves at Newport News.

The "500," Robert R. Young's steam turbine locomotive that was designed to thwart the ascendency of diesel-electric power and save the day for propulsion by coal, leaves Staunton, Virginia, in November of 1947. A steam yard switcher waits on a siding. To the disappointment of old-time railroad men and nostalgic railfans, the turbines didn't work out, and a few years later the C&O capitulated.

It is a little after three A.M., and the C&O passenger station in
Staunton is deserted except for a couple of trainmen, who are waiting
for No. 3, the Fast Flying Virginian, to arrive on the tracks to the
right, unload and take on passengers and mail, and resume its run to
Craigsville, Clifton Forge, Covington, and points west. Spring 1947.

Properly equipped with aluminum streamlined cowling, a 4–6–4
steam locomotive stands by at the Union Station in Washington, D.C.,
to haul the Washington section of the C&O's train of trains, No. 1, the
George Washington, 115 miles to Charlottesville, Virginia, at which
point more powerful equipment will replace it for the overnight run
westward across the mountains to Cincinnati and the Midwest.
August 1947.

At Fulton Yards in Richmond, a C&O 2–8–2 Mikado leaves for the
James River Division and Clifton Forge in June of 1948 with a train
of empty hopper cars.

Even with a pair of 4–8–4 Greenbriers at the head end and an old
articulated Mallet shoving from behind the caboose, it was not until
this low-slung, powerful 0–8–0 switcher's tractive effort was added to
the Mallet's a little later on that hot evening in July of 1948 that a long
train of loaded hopper cars could be made to move up the grade east
from Fulton Yards in Richmond.

The fireman turns a valve and the road foreman of engines looks on in
the cab of an older C&O Mallet pushing a coal train up the grade east
of Fulton yards in Richmond. Four tries and the addition of a switch
engine behind the Mallet were required to get it over the hill and
headed for Newport News. July 1948.

The C&O's Sportsman, with a 4–8–2 Mountain locomotive up front, having arrived from Newport News and picked up additional coaches, waits at the Main Street Station in Richmond in May 1947, for the signal to head west. The station's design was unusual. The tracks and train shed were elevated, with the Seaboard Air Line's through trackage along the west side and the C&O's along the east side of the shed, while trains originating at Richmond departed from beneath the shed itself.

Norfolk and Western compound articulated locomotive 2–8–8–2 No. 2160, a Y-6 Mallet, arrives at Roanoke, Virginia, with a train from the east in July of 1947.

Union Station, Roanoke, July 1947: The Powhatan Arrow leaves for the west behind a J-class 4–8–4 steam locomotive.

At Waynesboro, Virginia, N&W's train No. 13 from Hagerstown, Maryland, southward to Roanoke on the Shenandoah Division, pulled by a 4–8–2, waits on the lower level, while C&O's No. 5, the Sportsman, westbound to Staunton, Clifton Forge, and the Midwest, is at the upper level. The date is April 1947, and the 1937 Plymouth coupe parked to the right of the picture happens to be my first car.

Right: An 2–8–8–2 N&W H-6 Mallet pulls a freight train westward alongside the Appomattox River near Petersburg, Virginia, in May 1948.

A Virginian Railway 2–6–6–6 Mallet brings a train into Roanoke
in July 1947.

In January of 1948 this light 2–6–6–2 N&W Mallet was moving slowly through Luray, Virginia, on the Shenandoah Division, handling a way freight train. But I remember just such a locomotive that came bolting out of nowhere past a grade crossing at Luray at about eleven o'clock on a dark summer evening, doing at least sixty.

West of Roanoke the Virginian Railway hauled coal from the mines into Roanoke along electrified trackage with these box-cab locomotives. The Virginian was the only Class I railroad on which the freight trains had priority even over the passenger runs. July 1947.

A Virginian 2–8–2 yard engine with a load of empties, Roanoke, July 1947. Built as a single entity in the early 1900s to haul coal, the Virginian was laid out from mountains to Tidewater with as advantageous and straight an eastbound gradient as possible, and with no effort made to alter the course of the right-of-way in order to secure local traffic by serving cities and towns along the route. Ultimately the road merged with the N&W.

Not until the Norfolk and Western Railway began buying diesel-electric locomotives in the late 1950s would the Southern Railway have been permitted to utilize its own EMDs on N&W trackage, as in this photograph of the Birmingham Special coming through Bonsack, Virginia, in 1959. Until then, a steam locomotive would have been installed at the head end with the diesel units riding deadhead.

Left: One of the Virginian's powerful Lima-built 2–6–6–6 articulated Mallets at a water tower in the Roanoke yards, July 1947.

Ivy City yards, Washington, D.C., June 1947: Lined up and prepared to move down to Union Station to power outbound passenger trains are Pennsylvania GG-1's, Richmond, Fredericksburg and Potomac 4–8–4 Northerns, and, partially visible, a Baltimore and Ohio diesel.

They were efficient, handsome, and, once you had grown accustomed
to watching one GG-1 after another go by along the Pennsylvania's
Northeast Corridor, monotonous to look at. The Raymond Loewy-
designed electrics could do a hundred miles an hour hauling passenger
and freight trains along the electrified line between New York City and
Washington and from Philadelphia to Harrisburg. This one is bringing
a D.C.-bound train into Penn Station, Baltimore, in June 1948.

More interesting to watch, if only because scarcer, were the Pennsylvania's
box-cab electric freight locomotives, such as this one passing through
Penn Station, Baltimore, June 1948.

The Pennsylvania 4–4–2 Atlantics were relatively stubby, powerfully built locomotives. This one is departing from Penn Station in Baltimore with commuter coaches for Parktown on the non-electrified trackage to Harrisburg in June 1948.

This Baldwin "Centipede" diesel-electric, seen at Penn Station, Baltimore, in June 1948, pulled connecting passenger sections from Washington between Baltimore and Harrisburg, where they could be added to trains such as the Penn Texas, the Trail Blazer, and the St. Louisan.

A Baltimore and Ohio 2–10–2 Santa Fe–type steam locomotive at
Martinsburg, West Virginia, in January 1948.

Westward past Sykesville, Maryland, a Baltimore and Ohio 2–8–2 Mikado with Vanderbilt-type tender hauls freight along the old main line, on which steam railroading began in the United States. October 1948.

I drove into the B&O station at Hancock, Maryland, late on a
dark winter afternoon in January 1948, and shortly thereafter this
EMD E-6 came snaking around a curve with a Washington-bound
local passenger train.

Point of Rocks, Maryland, on the Potomac River, is where the B&O's main line from Washington and the old main line from Baltimore met. A 2–8–2 Mikado is pulling a freight train past the steepled station eastward to Baltimore. Another was at the rear of the train, pushing from behind the caboose. Spring 1949.

The B&O's all-coach Columbian—it did include a Slumber-coach—
left Washington at 4:30 P.M. and arrived in Chicago just over sixteen
hours later. Note the single dome car as it glides through Port of
Rocks, Maryland, on a rainy afternoon in early 1948.

A B&O 2–8–2 Mikado moves out of the Wilmington, Delaware, yards
with a train of empty hopper cars in July 1949.

Herewith the 4–4–0 of the Ma and Pa—the Maryland and Pennsylvania Railroad—which left Baltimore each afternoon with a coach-and-baggage-car train for York, Pennsylvania, 77 miles away, and got there in just over four hours. Built by Alco in Richmond in 1901, it had to go slow, because the Ma and Pa's right-of-way was apparently surveyed and constructed for narrow-gauge railroading, then before operations actually began the authorities opted instead for standard four-foot, eight-and-a-half-inch gauge. Note the two-axle caboose. The Pennsylvania's route required twenty fewer miles and two-and-a-half fewer hours to link Baltimore and York, but it wasn't nearly as much fun.

The Western Maryland Railroad operated a few commuter trains out of Baltimore in the late 1940s. This one, leaving Penn Station behind a 4–6–2 Pacific, was outbound to Glyndon and stations west on an autumn day in 1948.

A Reading Company 4–6–2 Pacific passenger locomotive at
Allentown, Pennsylvania, in July 1949.

A Lehigh Valley 2–8–2 Mikado lifts a heavy plume of coal smoke as it
pulls a freight train eastward through Allentown in July 1949.

Leaving the ornately towered station at Allentown, the Lehigh Valley's Black Diamond, with parlor cars and coaches, is bound for New York behind a two-unit Alco diesel in July 1949.

Past the passenger station at Pottstown moves a Reading Railway
Electro-Motive F-7 diesel pulling a freight train. July 1949.

This quite small 4–6–2 locomotive, built in 1911, hauled a daily
train from Knoxville, Tennessee, 35 miles up to Sevierville, when
photographed not far from the University of Tennessee campus in
December 1947. It is reported to be still in existence.

2–8–2 Mikado locomotive No. 1544, a Louisville and Nashville J-3, is at the head of a freight train in the L&N's Knoxville, Tennessee, yards. The locomotive at the water tower is No. 1334, a 2–8–0 Consolidation. December 1947.

In 1947, when this photo was taken at Chattanooga, Tennessee, the Nashville, Chattanooga and St. Louis Railroad was still separately operated, though largely owned by the Louisville and Nashville. The locomotive is an NC&StL 2–8–2 Mikado, arriving at the Chattanooga yards with a freight train.

This EMD E-7 diesel, about to leave the depot at Chattanooga for
Atlanta with the Georgian in December 1947, was owned by the
Louisville and Nashville but given the initials of both the L&N and
the Nashville Chattanooga and St. Louis on its nameplate. The L&N
held a controlling interest in the NC&StL, and in 1957 the two roads
were formally merged.

As all Civil War buffs know, Chattanooga, Tennessee, was a railroad center—the Louisville and Nashville, the Southern and various affiliates, the Nashville Chattanooga and St. Louis, the Central of Georgia, the Tennessee Alabama and Georgia—with main lines radiating out in five directions, to Cincinnati, Knoxville, Memphis, Atlanta, and Birmingham. It was also a center for iron foundries. With mountains surrounding it on three sides, the city was a very smoky place, as indicated by this photograph taken from a bridge over the Southern yards in December 1947. The railroads have long since gone diesel, and the iron foundries have mostly gone out of business. The mountains are still there, and recently when I crossed over the same bridge the air was crystal clear and the towers of downtown Chattanooga fully visible.

The Chesapeake Western, which provided freight service between Elkton, Harrisonburg, and Staunton, Virginia, in the Shenandoah Valley, was the surviving segment of the railroad that in the late 1860s. General Robert E. Lee envisioned being built up the Valley to Lexington and on to Roanoke, or Big Lick as it was then called. Later operated by the Southern, when I photographed this Baldwin end-cab switcher in Staunton in March 1947, the CW's affiliation was primarily with the Norfolk and Western. It owned three of these diesel locomotives.

When the Southern Railway declined to renew its lease on the line between Danville and Portsmouth, Virginia, along the Virginia–North Carolina border, in 1949, the Atlantic and Danville ownership set out to operate independently. Its old 2–8–0 Consolidations were replaced by new 1500-hp. Alco-GE road-switchers like this one, preparing to pull an overnight freight train from Danville to the tidewater in June 1950. Later mergers rendered the A&D superfluous in the scheme of things, and much of its trackage has now been uprooted.

My only opportunity to photograph an actual working wood-burner—
and I blew it. Around a bend in Rupert, West Virginia, on narrow-
gauge tracks in the summer of 1953, came several flat cars being
pushed by this Heisler, belonging to the Meadow River Lumber
Company. I was so excited that I failed to get my camera lens into
proper focus; thus this blurred image.

Henry Ford developed the Detroit, Toledo and Ironton Railroad to
fetch coal directly from the coal fields beyond the Ohio River to the
Model-T factories in Michigan. This formidable 2–8–2 Mikado was
shuffling the cars of a way freight at Washington Court House, Ohio,
in June 1951.

When diesel road locomotives replaced the cab-forward 4–8–8–2 oil-burning Mallets, the Southern Pacific operations people promptly removed all the water towers from stations along the Sunset Route to make sure the management wouldn't change its mind. Here in February 1954, not long after the changeover, a three-unit Alco diesel unit pulling the Sunset Limited waits at Del Rio, on the Texas-Mexican border, before commencing the long, long uphill journey to El Paso.

Coal-powered 4–6–2 Pacifics were still hauling local commuter trains out of San Jose, California, when this photo was made in February of 1954.

An Electro-Motive diesel pulls a passenger train of the Saint Louis–
San Francisco Railroad from the Union Station in St. Louis, in late
1954. More railroads, large and small, operated passenger service
from this station than from any other in the United States.

This Milwaukee Road 0–6–0 switcher was spotting cars along the
lakefront at Madison, Wisconsin, in June 1951.

A southbound Chicago and Northwestern streamliner powered by an
EMD diesel slips along the lake front into Madison, June 1951.

Right: The Canadian National was still operating steam locomotives
on its mainline trains when this 2–8–0 Consolidation brought a freight
train into Hamilton, Ontario, in August 1954.

An 0–6–0 Canadian National switching locomotive at work in
Hamilton, Ontario, in August 1954.

Two diesel road-switcher units move a freight train past the Grand
Trunk Western station in Lansing, Michigan, in August 1954. Further
up the line is a steam locomotive, but although I waited at the station
for a half-hour it declined to approach any nearer.

South of Denver along the Colorado and Southern tracks a Burlington 2–8–2 Mikado heads for Texas with a freight train, the Rocky Mountains for backdrop, late in 1954.

Right: Steam locomotion survived on the Union Pacific's Kansas City-Denver run well after it disappeared from off the main line through Omaha. This shot was taken from the vestibule of the rear car of the Portland Rose west of Kansas City as the 4–8–4 Northern led the train onto a siding on a rainy morning in the fall of 1954.

The Iron Horse leaves the UP trail. This melancholy scene, photographed from a viaduct over the Union Pacific yards at Cheyenne, Wyoming, in late 1954, shows a string of steam locomotives, of varying age and stages of dismantlement, lined up on two tracks to await the eventual deadhead journey to the scrapyard.

Rescued! Not until decades later, when I was writing this book, did I learn that the pert ten-wheeler with the spark arrester on its stack, steam locomotive No. 1242, did not suffer the fate of the Big Boys and other Union Pacific behemoths that I photographed lined up for scrapping at Cheyenne in 1954. No. 1242, originally No. 1476 and built by Cooke Locomotive Works in Paterson, New Jersey, in 1890, had been hauling mixed trains for thirty-three years on the UP's Walcott, Saratoga and Encampment run in the south Wyoming high country, until displaced early in 1954. Soon after I photographed it in the yards, it was moved to Lions Park in Cheyenne to be on public exhibition. After thirty-six years of growing neglect there, it was restored to its onetime comeliness for the Laramie County Centennial in 1990 and is now on display.

A trail of white-and-gray coal smoke drifts along the Kansas prairie in the wake of a 4–8–4 Northern locomotive pulling the Portland Rose westbound for Denver from Kansas City on the UP in 1954. The smoke will swiftly dissolve, and very soon steam railroading will be gone from the land.

Works Consulted

Cox, Fletcher. *The Complete Steam Locomotive Companion.* Alexandria, Va.: Thoughts in Focus, *n.d.*

Foster, Gerald. *A Field Guide to Trains of North America.* Boston: Houghton Mifflin, 1996.

Hubbard, Freeman. *Encyclopedia of North American Railroading.* New York: McGraw-Hill, 1981.

Kennedy, George. "Some Famous Trains," in Louis D. Rubin, Jr., ed., *A Writer's Companion.* Harper Perennial ed., rev. New York: HarperCollins, 1997.

Kratville, William W. *Steam, Steel & Limiteds.* Omaha, Neb.: Kratville, 1983.

Morgan, David P., ed. *Steam's Finest Hour.* Milwaukee, Wis.: Kalmbach, 1959.

Official Guide of the Railways. New York: National Railway Publishing Company. Published monthly. Volumes for February 1931 and May 1958.

Stover, John F. *The Life and Decline of the American Railroad.* New York: Oxford University Press, 1970.

Turner, Charles W., Thomas W. Dixon, Jr., and Eugene L. Huddleston. *Chessie's Road.* Second edition. Alderson, W.Va.: Chesapeake & Ohio Historical Society, 1986.

Index

Bristol, Va.-Tenn., 21, 58
Broad Street Station, Richmond, 5–6, 39, **61**, **69**, **95**
Brodie, Steve, 92
Bryan, Ohio, 57, **104**
Bryant, William Cullen, 50
Buggs Island reservoir, Va.-N.C., 42
Burlington Lines, 34, 56–57, **168**

C&O. *See* Chesapeake and Ohio
Camden Station, Baltimore, Md., 37
camelback locomotives, 8, **107**
Camp Gordon, Ga., 3
Canadian National Railways, 57, **165–66**
Canadian Pacific Railway, 57
Cape Charles, Va., 38
Carnegie Corporation, 55
Carolina Special (Southern Railway), 14, **82**
"Casey Jones" (song), 53
Centralia, Mo., 54
Central of Georgia Railway, 155
Central Railroad of New Jersey. *See* Jersey Central
Champions, East and West Coast (Atlantic Coast
    Line), 5, 11
Chancellorsville, battle of, 40
Charleston, College of, 3
Charleston, S.C., 3–5, 7–8, 10–18, 23, 44ff., 59–60, **68**,
    79
Charlotte, N.C., 47
Charlottesville, Va., 20, 28, **85**, **114–15**, 119
Chattanooga, Tenn., 28–29, **153–55**
Chesapeake and Ohio canal, 46
Chesapeake and Ohio Railway, 10, 19ff., 30–32, 39–40,
    46, 57; operations at Afton, Va., 20, **113**; Char-
    lottesville, Va., 20, 28, **114–15**, 119; Clifton Forge,
    20–21, 24–25, 57, **110–12**, 118, 120, 126;
    Doswell, Va., 10, 90, 92; Glasgow, Va., **116**; New-
    port News, 20, 30–33, 115, 122–123; Richmond,
    Va., 20, 22ff., 38, 41, 57, 115–16, **120–22**;
    Staunton, Va., 19ff., 27ff., **117–18**, 126, 156;
    Washington, D.C., 20, 25, **119**; Waynesboro, Va.,
    20, 22, **108–9**, **126**; trains—Chessie, 25–26; FFV,

20, 23–24, 118; George Washington, 20, 22–23,
26–27, **119**; Sportsman, 19–20, 23, 27–28, 39,
108, **120**, **126**; "500" steam turbine locomotive,
25–26, **117**; Church Hill tunnel cave-in, 41;
Robert R. Young and, 24–26; 117; merges with
Baltimore and Ohio to become Chessie System,
60; becomes part of CSX, 60
Chesapeake Western Railroad, 23, **156**
Chessie's Road (Turner, Dixon, and Huddleston), 173
Chessie System, merges with Seaboard Coast Line to
    form CSX, 60
Chessie (Chesapeake and Ohio), 25–26
Cheyenne, Wyo., 57
Chicago and Northwestern Railroad, 34, 53, **164**
Chicago, Burlington and Quincy. *See* Burlington Lines
Chicago, Ill., 27–28, 37, 54, 142
Chicago, Milwaukee, St. Paul and Pacific. *See* Milwau-
    kee Road
Chicago, Rock Island and Pacific Railroad. *See* Rock
    Island Lines
Church Hill Tunnel cave-in, 41
Cincinnati, Ohio, 21, 27–28, 53–55, 57, 119
Citadel, The, 16, 18
City of San Francisco (Union Pacific), 56
City of St. Louis (Wabash), 54
Civil War, 29, 35, 38, 40, 42, 51, 83, 155
Clarksville, Va., 42
Clemens, Samuel L., 22
Clifton Forge, Va., 20–21, 24–25, 57, **110–12**, 118,
    120, 126
Clio, S.C., 49
Colorado and Southern, 168
Columbia, Mo., 54
Columbia, S.C., 3–5, 14, 17, 19, 32, **82**
Columbus, Ga., 3
Complete Steam Locomotive Companion (Cox), 173
Cooke Locomotive Works ten-wheeler, **170–71**
Cooper River, 18, 51–52
Cooper River Bridge, Charleston, S.C., 51
Covington, Va., 118
Cox, Fletcher, 173

Craigsville, Va., 118
CSX system, 2, 60. *See also* Atlantic Coast Line; Baltimore and Ohio; Chesapeake and Ohio; Chessie System; Seaboard Air Line; Seaboard Coast Line
Cumberland, Md., 53–54

Danville, Va., 28, 41–43, 83, **157**
Davis, Jefferson, 42, 83
Del Rio, Tex., 55, **160**
Delaware, Lackawanna and Western Railroad. *See* Lackawanna Railroad
Delaware Water Gap, 106
Delmarva peninsula, 38
Delta Air Lines, 3
Denniston, Va., 42
Denver and Rio Grande Western Railroad, 56
Denver, Colo., 56–57, **168**, 169, 172
Des Moines Rocket (Rock Island), 56
Detroit, Mich., 59, 159
Detroit, Toledo and Ironton Railroad, 53, **159**
Dillon, S.C., 49–50, **79**
Dixon, Thomas W., Jr., 25–26, 173
Doswell, Va., 10, 39, **89–92**, **94**
Durbin, W.Va., 54

Eastern Shore, 38–39
East Lansing, Mich., 57
Edison, Thomas Alva, 57, 167
Electro-Motive diesel locomotives, 28–29, 46–47, 53, 57–58, **64–65**, **69**, **71**, **80–81**, **133**, **150**
Elizabeth River, 42–43
Elkins, W.Va., 54
Elkton, Va., 58, 156
El Paso, Tex., 55–56, 160
EMD. *See* Electro-Motive locomotives
Emmitsburg, Md., 37
Emporia, Va., 43
Encyclopedia of North American Railroading (Hubbard), 173
Engle, Paul, 34
Erie Railroad, 7–8, **96–98**

Esmont, Va., 40
"Express, The" (Spender), 35

Farragut, David G., 51
Fast Flying Virginian. *See* FFV
Federation for Railway Progress, 24
FFV (C&O), 20, 23–25, 118
Field Guide to Trains of North America, A (Foster), 173
Flagler, Henry M., 11
Florida East Coast Railway, 11
Florida Special (Atlantic Coast Line), 15
Ford, Henry, 53
Fort Benning, Ga., 3, 47
Fort Drum, N.Y., 4
Fort McClellan, Ala., 9, 35
Foster, Gerald, 173
Foster, Stephen, 50
France, 59
Franklin, Va., 43
Fredericksburg, Va., 9, 40
French National Railways, 8
Frisco Line. *See* St. Louis-San Francisco
Fulton Yards, Richmond, Va., 28, 30–31, 41, **120–22**

Gaithersburg, Md., 29
General, The (locomotive), 29
Georgetown, S.C., 50
George Washington (C&O), 20, 22–23, 26–27, **119**
Georgian, The (L&N-NC&StL), 29, **154**
Gibson, N.C., 49
"Girl from Red Lion, Pa., The" (Mencken), 37
Glasgow, Va., 116
Glyndon, Md., 146
Golden Apples, The (Welty), 43–44
Grahame, Kenneth, 3
Grand Central Terminal, 4
Grand Trunk Western Railroad, 57, **167**
Great Lakes, 53
Great Salt Lake, Utah, 56
Greeley, Colo., 56–57
Gresham, S.C., 50

Savannah River, 15

Savannah, Ga., 14–16, 48ff., 63, 75–76, 79

Schenectady, N.Y., 8, 99

Schuyler, Va., 40

Seaboard Air Line Railway, 3–6, 58–68; operations at Andrews, S.C., 50–51, **78**; Charleston, S.C., 4–5, 11, 16–18, 45–52, **75**; Charlotte, N.C., 47; Columbia, S.C., 3–5, 17; Dillon, S.C., 48–49, **79**; Hamlet, N.C., 1, 4–5, 45–52, 59, 75, **76–77**; Petersburg, Va., 47, **73**, **81**; Raleigh, N.C., 59–60; Richmond, Va., 5–6, 39, 45–46, **70–72**, 77, **80**, 123; Wilmington, N.C., 47–48, 76–77; trains— Boll Weevil, 4–5, 7–8, 15–18, 44–52, 59, **75**, 76; Silver Meteor, 3–5, 45–47, 59–60; Silver Star, 5; merges with Atlantic Coast Line to become Seaboard Coast Line, 58–60. *See also* CSX; Seaboard Coast Line

Seaboard Coast Line, 58–60; merges with Chessie System to become CSX, 59–60

Secaucus, N.J., 8, **96**

Selma, N.C., 60

Seviersville, Tenn., 29, 151

Shenandoah Valley, Va., 19ff., 28–29, 58

Sicily, 58

Silver Meteor (Seaboard Air Line), 3–5, 45–47, 59–60

Silver Star (Seaboard Air Line), 5

"Slabs of the Sunburnt West" (Sandburg), 55

Smith, R. H., 59

Smoky Mountain Railroad, 29, **151**

Snapp, Ben, 25

"Song of Marion's Men, The" (Bryant), 50

Southern Pacific Lines, 55–56, **160–61**

Southern Railway, 21, 25, 27–28, 40–42, 58, 133; operations at Bristol, Va.-Tenn., 58; Charleston, S.C., 11–12, 14–15, 18, **84**; Charlottesville, Va., 27–28, **85**; Chattanooga, Tenn., 29, **155**; Columbia, S.C., 14, **82**; Lexington, Ky., **87**; Lynchburg, Va., 19, 28, **85**; Summerville, S.C., 5; Richmond, Va., 46, **83**, **86**; St. George, S.C., 60; trains – Birmingham Special, 58, **133**; Carolina Special, 14, **82**; Royal Palm, **87**; Tennessean, 58; Washington-Atlanta-New Orleans Express, 42; and Atlantic and Danville Railway, 157; and Chesapeake Western, 156; merges with Norfolk and Western to become Norfolk Southern, 60

South Hill, Va., 43

Spender, Stephen, 35

Sportsman, The (C&O), 19–20, 23, 27–28, 39, **108**, **120**, **126**

Springfield, Ohio, 53

Standard Oil Company of New Jersey, 22

Staunton News-Leader, 19ff., 29–30

Staunton, Va., 19ff., 27ff., **117–18**, 126, **156**

Steam turbine locomotives, 25–26, **117**

Steam's Finest Hour (Morgan), 173

Steel, Steam and Limiteds (Kratville), 173

Stover, John C., 57, 173

Suffolk, Va., 43

Summerville, S. C.. 13–15

Sunset Limited (Southern Pacific), 55–56, **160**

Susquehanna Railroad, 7–8, **105**

Susquehanna Transfer, N.J., 105

Sykesville, Md., **140**

Teaneck, N.J., 5, **101**

Tennessean (Southern Railway), 58

Tennessee Georgia and Alabama Railroad, 155

Tennessee, University of, 29

Toano, Va., 32

Toledo, Ohio, 53

Trail Blazer (Pennsylvania), 138

Trains Magazine, 5–6, 41–43

Turner, Charles W., 173

Twain, Mark, 22

Union City, N. J., 7

Union Pacific Railroad, 34, 56–57; at Cheyenne, Wyo., **169–71**; near Kansas City, Mo., **169**, **172**; Portland Rose, **169**, **172**

Uniontown, Pa., 53–54